Stand Up!

Bobby Knoxall

Stand Up!

The amazing life story of one of Britain's funniest comics and his hilarious encounters with world famous stars

Published by Ghostwriters UK Ltd, PO Box 763, Sunderland, SR2 7XR

First published in hardback in 2003
ISBN 0-9542109-2-1

Printed in Great Britain by Tandem Press
www.tandempress.com

All photographs published by kind permission of Bobby Knoxall, Patrick Lavelle and The Sunderland Echo. Every attempt has been made to contact the relevant copyright-holders, but some were unobtainable. We would be grateful if the appropriate people could contact Ghostwriters UK Ltd.

Ghostwriters UK Ltd is a writers' publishing co-operative.

For my lovely wife Diane and for Ken Wayne, the man who, more than most, taught me all I needed to know about surviving in show-business

Contents

Acknowledgements

Special thanks go to my biographer Patrick Lavelle, to my wife Diane and my friend Joe Foster, who helped with research. Thanks are also due to my friends Jackie Longstaff and Bill Tipling, to my fellow comedian Alan Fox, to Miles Knox, Matt Roseberry, George Craig, Sammy Doran, Tommy Conroy, Adrian Marshall and others who contributed to my life story.

Foreword

I've been a big fan of Bobby Knoxall ever since I was a young lad.

I was a welder at the Caterpillar Factory in Birtley, Tyneside, was coming to the end of my apprenticeship and, I must admit, I didn't like it all.

All I wanted to be, like Bobby Knoxall, was a comedian.

I remember one morning the lads at work had been to see Bobby and said he was brilliant.

I first saw him at The Ouston Social Club in Chester-le-Street, County Durham, and I laughed until my belly was aching. It was 1974 and I was then 21.

Bobby oozes confidence, from the moment he walks on stage. He makes you feel as if you are in his front room.

A lot of people nowadays say to me that they wouldn't mind being an actor, or that they'd like to be one. In my opinion wanting to be something isn't good enough... you have to need to be.

I know Bobby has always needed to be a comedian. That's his passion in life.

This comes out in the delivery of his lines and in his 100 per cent belief in his material. That's what makes him so special.

I learnt after my short spell in the clubs that my own favourite joke might not be the audience's favourite, but with Bobby, every gag he tells sounds like his favourite, no question about it, and he delivers them brilliantly.

He has travelled all over the world making people laugh and you have to care about people to want to do that.

I have a great respect for this man and I was flattered when he suggested I might want to write the foreword to his life story. I've never written nowt in a book before.

I'm a fan. I must admit I nicked a couple of his gags when I was starting out; I just didn't tell them as well as he can.

Bobby is a one-off, a comedian's comedian. He'll always be a legend in the North East and his humour travels across the world.

He's just fought through a life-threatening operation and has bounced back and is performing his own unique brand of humour again.

I take my hat off to you, pal, wish you love and luck, and I know people young and old who buy this book will have a great read.

PS: I would have put a tenner in with this letter... but it was sealed up!

God bless you.

Tim Healy

Preface

Bobby Knoxall, one of Britain's best stand-up comedians, was on his death bed when he started telling me his life story.

It was the story of a man with a natural gift; the gift of being able to make people laugh.

He was born into a large family living in abject poverty in the tough East End of Sunderland in North East England and it was this upbringing that gave him his hard edge; the edge to survive and earn a decent living for himself and his family in the toughest profession in show-business on the toughest stage most comedians have ever known – the working-men's club circuit.

But Bobby – unlike some other equally well-known comedians in the North East – did not restrict himself to his home territory. His talent took him all over the world, from Jersey to Zambia, Rhodesia, South Africa, the Middle East, the Far East, Australia, and in Europe to Spain, Italy, Germany and many other foreign countries.

During his 50 years in show-business he mixed with, and starred alongside, some of the world's biggest stars; Ella Fitzgerald, Matt Munro, Charlton Heston, Rocky Marciano, Roy Orbison, to name but a few, and shared the bill with many household-name comedians such as Tommy Cooper, Freddie Starr, Ken Dodd, Bernard Manning, Frank Carson, Russ Abbott, Bob Monkhouse, Les Dawson, Tom O'Connor, Harry H Corbett, Marti Caine, his good friend Mike Reid, of Eastenders fame, and many more.

He has earned millions and spent tens of thousands on booze, cigarettes, gambling and women. He has had love affairs with a top soap star, the daughter of one of the world's top singing stars, a Eurovision Song Contest winner, and more strippers and cabaret dancers than he cares to remember.

One of his London agents was a good friend of the Kray Twins and one of his North East agents was the accountant for a gaming boss who disappeared following a notorious gangland shooting and remained on Interpol's most wanted list for almost 12 years.

Gangsters and would-be gangsters were drawn to him, fellow comedians watched his stage-show in awe and, sometimes, trepidation, and agents who messed with him felt the full force of his anger. Bobby Knoxall knocked them out

But throughout his roller-coaster, globe-trotting, star-spangled, career, Bobby Knoxall's feet – unless he was standing up and kicking someone in the head – remained firmly on the ground.

And wherever he travelled, he always returned home, to Sunderland; the city in which he was born and grew up, and the city he loves so much.

For every pound Bobby Knoxall has wasted, he has raised two pounds for charities. Hospitals have been provided with new, life-saving equipment, terminally-ill youngsters have fulfilled their dying wishes, and some hospital patients who could now be dead, are living fruitful, and thankful, lives.

It was Bobby's love of his hometown, and his desire to do what he wanted, that stopped him from becoming a national celebrity in the UK. National stardom is something he has never desired.

But it's about time his comic talent was truly recognised and for his charity work I expect his name – if there's any justice in this world – to soon be on the New Year's Honours List.

Patrick Lavelle
October 2003

Chapter One
THE DEATH BED

"What's my chances, doc?" I asked, as I lay on the bed. "And can you give it to me straight?"

The doctor, his stethoscope hanging from his neck, was looking at my chart at the foot of the bed, jotting down a few notes. He raised his eyes to look at me and paused for a second.

"You have an aneurysm in your stomach, Bobby," he said.

"Most aneurysms are five to seven inches long and can quite routinely be operated on."

"Right," I said. "So it just means an operation?"

"It's not as simple as that, Bobby," the doctor said. "Your aneurysm is almost 22 inches long. It may be inoperable. If we can operate, and there's no guarantee, it will be a very risky operation."

"What's my chances, though?" I asked again.

"No more than seventy thirty," the doctor said.

"That's not bad," I said.

"That is bad," the doctor said, "because you're the thirty."

Had it been someone else lying on the hospital bed, I could have easily delivered a quick punchline, a quick one-liner that would have produced a few muffled laughs and eased the tension in the room.

But there was nothing funny at having just been told you're more than likely to die very soon.

My wife Diane, sitting at the side of the bed resting her head in her hand, was staring straight at me and her beautiful eyes were welling up with tears. She had heard what the doctor had to say and, after he left the room, we sat there holding each other's hand in stunned silence.

I'd never died before. Well, only once, in my career.

I'd known a few comedians that had died a death more than once, on stages up and down the country, in the sense that they had bombed, failed to raise a laugh, failed to connect with the audience.

I had never thought my time would come lying in a hospital bed. I had always thought – even desired – that I would literally die on stage, die with my boots on, still making people laugh right up to my last living moment.

My brother Charlie entered the room and Diane went to meet him, standing in a corner, repeating in whispers what we had just been told by the doctor.

"Fuck that!" Shouted Charlie. "Fuck it! There must be something they can do. You've raised thousands for this bloody hospital."

"Calm down," I said, but my voice was too weak for the sound to be carried just a few feet to register in the mind of my volatile brother. He had obviously taken the news badly.

"We'll go private," he said. "We'll raise the money and go private."

Of course, it had nothing to do with money. If money was the answer they would have found a cure for cancer and Steve McQueen wouldn't have died when he did.

This aneurysm stretched from just below my neck to my lower abdomen and for months it had been poisoning my body and my brain.

What caused it was a mystery but something had to be done. I was told it could burst at any time and when it did that would be it. Finito, time to push up the daisies and go to that big comedy club in the sky where everything's a laugh a minute and there's never any sign of a heckler.

It was all very strange, because I felt reasonably fit, even though I had lost about five stone in weight. I was still doing the business on stage, mainly at charity nights and sportsmen's dinners, cracking all my best gags, arranging all the acts, and acting, as always, as Master of Ceremonies. It wasn't exactly a punishing schedule, just the odd night of the week, and I felt fine.

I hadn't really noticed the loss of appetite and the resulting weight loss, or the fact that off-stage I was talking a load of crap, a load of gibberish, stringing sentences together that made no sense at all to anyone around me, but appeared to make sense to me. I hadn't shown any symptoms associated with this killer inside my belly, this abdominal aortic aneurysm; no rhythmic throbbing in my guts, no hypertension. I did feel a little bunged up. I just thought that was constipation.

But someone had noticed a big change in me, my wife Diane, and she was worried. For a time she and my sister Violet thought I was developing Alzheimer's Disease. There had to be a reason I sometimes talked nonsense and sometimes didn't even recognise members of my own family.

It was at Diane's insistence that I visited the family GP, but he could find no problem. It was Diane who practically dragged me to Sunderland General Hospital's accident and emergency unit and demanded I sit around for a few hours in the waiting room to find out what the problem was. I had never known my wife to be so persistent, but she was absolutely convinced there was something wrong with me, despite my best efforts at reassuring her that everything was all right in the Knoxall camp.

Whilst waiting to see the doctor I was gripped by a spasm, which made my body shake and my eyes glaze over. It was when the doctor asked me who the Queen was and then pointed to Diane and asked me who she was, and I was unable to answer either of the questions, that the doctor quickly got me into a consulting room for a diagnosis. It was amazing the affect this aneurysm had on my mind, and even more amazing that it never affected my performance on stage.

My brother Charlie had calmed down a little before he left the hospital to spread the gloomy news to the rest of the family.

I was given a full body scan, returned to my hospital room and rested for a couple of hours. Diane still sat by my bedside and after another couple of hours the doctor returned.

"We can operate, Bobby," he said, "but I am going to have to fly in an anaesthetist with specialist experience from Amsterdam. The operation will last about seven hours and it is a painful operation."

"I'm not bothered about the pain. I can take it," I said.

"You will have to be strong, and if you're strong you can fight it," the doctor added.

I'd always been a fighter. I had sparked a few agents out in my time, mixed with some of the toughest bare-knuckle streetfighters, punched my way into and out of some clubs and kicked seven types of shit out of many people who stood in my way.

Now I faced the biggest battle of my life; the battle to survive.

Diane looked shell-shocked. The news had hit her hard, even though she had realised there was something wrong with me. It had never dawned on either of us that my life was under threat and that my chances of survival were pretty slim.

"What will you do?" I asked.

"What will I do if what?"

It was obvious the finality of it all was hitting home and it was something that Diane was having difficulty talking about. But the high probability that I was soon going to die was something that we needed to discuss. It wasn't the time to talk about what type of coffin I wanted to be laid to rest in and how many pall bearers would be required. It was time to talk about what Diane would do and, especially, what would happen to our four boys, Robert, John, Ryan and Brent.

"What will you do if I die?" I asked.

Diane started sobbing, quietly, hot tears running down her finely-sculpted features.

"I don't know," she said. "I don't belong here. I'm a Londoner and I'm only here because you're here. I don't really know many people in Sunderland; just the people you know."

As a family we had lived all over the world; wherever the work had taken me. Jersey, Rhodesia, Zambia, South Africa, Dubai, Abu Dhabi, Germany, Hong Kong, Bangkok. Living out of suitcases in some of the world's finest hotels with two of our boys, and with me performing virtually every night in some of the finest cabaret rooms across the globe. But we always ended up back in Sunderland, my hometown and the town we all called home.

Diane was born in East Ham and she was right, she only came to live in Sunderland because we were married and I wanted us to live in my hometown and bring up our family there.

"Would you move back to London?" I asked.

"I really don't know, Bob," she said. "Anyway, why are we talking like this. You're going to pull through it. I know you are."

Our sons, all fine, strapping, lads, were all Mackems – the name for a Wearsider as opposed to a Geordie from Newcastle – and proud of it. Their roots were in Sunderland and from those roots had grown relationships and friendships.

What would they do without their dad around?

Diane walked towards the window, looked out on to the Sunderland skyline, and plunged into deep thought. We'd been married for 30 years and she had been the one constant in my life. Until I met her I had lived quite a reckless life, full of heavy boozing, heavy gambling, heavy smoking, fighting and shagging every woman who made herself available. And there had been hundreds of women; cabaret dancers, strippers, a top television soap star, the daughter of one of the world's top singers, groupie-types and a club cleaner or two. I had shagged my way from the East End Social Club in Sunderland to the Crazy Horse cabaret room in The Beach Hotel in Durban. And I didn't give a damn.

But then I met Diane and my shagging days were over. I cut down on the booze and the gambling – but not the fags – and she brought some semblance of normality into my crazy life. Hers was a calming influence and with our marriage, and later our boys, came something that I had never accepted nor wanted before, responsibility.

"I could murder a fag," I said.

"It'll be a long time before you're allowed a cigarette," said Diane.

"Do you think this is it?" I asked.

"You're not going to die," she said. "You've got too much to live for."

I didn't share Diane's optimism.

I wasn't actually frightened of death, just fearful of the unknown. Was I destined for that paradise I had learned so much about in St Patrick's Roman Catholic Primary School in the East End of Sunderland? Or was I destined for the hell, fire and brimstone the nuns at the same school convinced me would be my fate if I did not reject Satan and repent for my sins?

My thoughts on the after-life were fleeting as I lay in the hospital bed. With what time I had left on my hands and time to think, it was time to take stock on what had gone before, on what I had achieved.

During my 50 years in show-business I had earned, and wasted, millions, mixed with world famous stars, met my wife Diane and travelled the globe.

And what did I have to show for it?

Not a penny.

We still lived in a two-bedroomed council house in the Farringdon area of Sunderland, I had no savings in the bank, no nest egg in the house.

But what I did have was something of more value than cash; a loving wife and family, a wide circle of true friends and some very precious memories of a life in the fast lane which had been full of colour, humour, passion, risk, danger and adventure.

On your death-bed, we are told, your life flashes by you. As I lay on the bed in Sunderland General Hospital I was only hours away from the operating theatre and only hours away from life or death.

My survival, I knew, would depend on the skill of the surgeon and on my own will to fight for my life.

As I was wheeled into the operating theatre, Diane walking with me and holding my hand, I wondered if I would ever see her again. Seeing her leave, after I was placed on to the operating table, was the most desperate moment I had encountered. My mind was racing.

After the anaesthetist plunged the huge needle into my spine, I slowly drifted into unconsciousness and my mind took me on a journey back in time, back to where it all began.

And as I battled for survival images came into my head of people I had known who had ended their life's journey and of others, still alive, for whom life was only just beginning.

I don't know if this was a near-death experience and I can't remember if I found myself floating near the ceiling looking down on myself in my hospital bed.

All I do know is that I had entered a very deep sleep, and one from which I thought I would never wake.

Chapter Two

THE WAR YEARS

My dad was shaking like a man possessed as my Aunt Lal stuffed her fingers in his mouth to stop him from swallowing his tongue and Uncle Mattie Jackson knelt on his chest trying to keep him still. He was foaming at the mouth like a rabid dog and his body jerked violently, his clenched fists hitting the air and his feet kicking out in all directions.

The wail of the air raid siren filled the still early evening air, as residents of St Patrick's Garth in Sunderland's East End rushed to the nearest shelter at Fenwick's Brewery and as I looked out from the veranda I saw the enemy plane in clear view, its Nazi insignia clearly visible, and flames shooting from its engine compartment.

The pilot appeared surprisingly calm as he prepared to bale out and I could hear hardly a sound as the plane slowly headed, nose down, towards the fish quay, leaving a vapour trail along the clifftops at Ryhope, Grangetown and Hendon in its wake.

"He's going to crash. He's going to crash, Uncle Matt," I shouted excitedly, but Uncle Matt was too busy trying to calm my dad John who was in the throes of one of his worst epileptic fits.

My dad, who had been in the Royal Navy, had been torpedoed during the war and came home half the man he used to be, suffering serious illness and these spasmodic epileptic seizures which were painful to witness.

"He's crashed, Uncle Matt. He's crashed," I said, after seeing the plane hit the deck and burst into flames not far from the water's edge in the dock. Its pilot and the navigator had somehow managed to eject and from my vantage point I could see them both running south, heading towards Hendon, with a couple of local wardens, and a number of Eastenders, in hot pursuit on foot.

Uncle Matt and Aunt Lal had managed to calm my dad. He had his arms around both of their shoulders as they led him to the front door of our flat, my mother Meggie bringing up the rear, pushing her arms into her old, threadbare coat.

"Eeeh, me teeth. I've forgot me teeth," said my mother, as she rushed back into the flat.

"For God's sake leave your teeth," said Uncle Matt, "they're dropping bombs, not fucking pies."

The panic inside the house gave way to the panic outside and we all headed for the air raid shelter, knowing we would probably be there for the rest of the night.

Night after night there were air raids in the town as Hitler's Luftwaffe swooped, dropping bombs indiscriminately on key targets, such as the shipyards, collieries and other areas where there were engineering works.

But with residential areas, such as The Garths in the East End, so close to industrial centres it was inevitable there would be heavy civilian casualties.

The house we lived in, in Hedworth Terrace, was bombed early in the war and one of my mother's legs was ripped open in the blast. She had to go into hospital for several weeks and the kids in the family had to move in with friends or relations.

The Garths, where my family moved to once my mother was well again, were Sunderland's answer to the East End slum clearance of the 1930s; square four-storey blocks with communal balconies, or verandas as we called them, and deck access to the mainly three-bedroom flats, each of the seven garths with an inner quadrangle where the kids would play and neighbours would congregate.

For many families The Garths provided them with homes with their first taste of relatively modern-day living, such as running water and indoor toilets.

I shared the flat in St Patrick's Garth with my mother and father, my sisters Pat, Angela and Violet (Karen came into the world much later) and my brothers Jonty, a thick-set fighter who took his hat off to no one, Charlie, Kenny and Harry. Harry was killed during the war in a tragic accident.

With so many of us living in what was a small flat, my bed was the bath and my blankets overcoats. New additions seem to come into the family about every two years and Jonty, my oldest brother, had to move out and in with our grandparents when he was 15, to give us all a little more room.

Poverty in the East End was widespread. Three scones with a cherry on top was what many families would call a wedding cake and impoverished parents with constipated toddlers who could not afford laxatives would put their kid on the potty and tell him or her ghost stories.

There were a lot of quiet weddings in The Garths, because the bride always wore sandshoes.

One of the families used to go to a nearby café and ask the owner to fill a jam jar full of hot tea. "Is that it?", the café boss would ask, to which came the reply: "No. Can I also have 13 straws?"

My dad, John Thomas McKenna, once told me the story about how a burglar broke into our house and he confronted him in the sitting room, where he was shining his torch. "What yer doing?" My dad asked. "I'm looking for cash and jewellery," the burglar said. "Then hang on, I'll turn the light on, and we'll both bloody look," my dad said.

Neighbours would knock on our door each morning and ask to borrow a cup of sugar, a cup of milk, or ask my mother to rub a bit soap on a manky flannel.

And the walls in the flat were thin, so thin we could often hear a couple next door having sex.

One time my mother opened the oven door to baste the Sunday roast – nothing more than a leg of mince - and found the fella next door dipping his bread into OUR gravy.

No one locked their front doors in the Garths. Who wanted to steal a mangle? There was a great sense of neighbourliness.

In front of all fires in the flats lay clippy mats, old pieces of cloth sewn together, and this was the only carpeting on the floor. But at least everyone had wall-to-wall floorboards.

My dad, like most men from the East End, would ride a bike to Hendon Beach most mornings and come back with a sackful of coal dust. He would form the dust into coal balls and use them, sparingly, on the open fire, then cough up the coal dust from his lungs and spit the mouthful which was all colours of the rainbow, into the hot grate, where it would sizzle and bubble and, eventually, dry out.

This type of poverty was rife in the East End long before the outbreak of the Second World War. The East End was home to a workhouse which was home, initially, to 600 paupers and in the early 1930s a Salvation Army Hostel opened in High Street East, providing food and accommodation for up to 130 men. The East End was also home to the Boys' Orphanage, which was known as the East End Boys' Orphan Asylum before the age of enlightenment, when the powers-that-be considered such a name might suggest the poor and destitute boys might be labelled insane.

Where there was no work for East End men and no hope for East End women, a thriving black market evolved, with daily dodgy deals on contraband or stolen goods and, from the desperation of abject poverty, emerged the twilight world of Sunderland's only red light area; but even then there was no red lights.

The ladies of the night plied their trade in the local pubs, The Ship Inn and The Bridge Hotel were among them, and there was a regular clientele; the sailors that arrived daily on ships entering the River Wear, on shore leave, with a pocketful of shillings, and looking for a cheap and easy lay.

So, when rationing came along, Eastenders were hit by a double-whammy. Improvisation was a byword, necessity was the mother of invention and the air raids, when they came, brought with them not fear and trepidation, but momentary relief from the daily drudgery and having to make ends meet.

"Oh, Danny Boy, the pipes, the pipes, are caw, aw, ling," was the sound that greeted us when we entered the air raid shelter inside Fenwick's Brewery.

"From glen to glen, and by the mountainside ..."

The old men of the parish, too old or too unfit for war – they were certainly not key workers – had tapped into the barrels and the beer was flowing freely.

And as the sirens wailed, and in the town's Anderson shelters families cowered in fear, in the East End – at least in our bomb shelter – folk were having a party.

It was the same when Pryde's Bakery was hit in Coronation Street, the street that ran by the top end of St Patrick's Garth. Pryde's prided itself on baking award-winning bread. In 1936 the firm won the national first prize for baking the best sandwich bread in the country.

The sandwich bread was, indeed, delicious – even when it was slightly smoke-damaged by fire during the blitz. The women of The Garths lined up for their partly-burned loaves of bread – a bit like a loaf of toast – and were thankful for it.

Joshua Wilson's, a wholesalers at the corner of Lombard Street and Queen Street, was another local food firm hit by fire. It was tragic for the owners, but for myself, my mate Tommy Reeves and the Young brothers, it was an opportunity. After the firemen had done all they could to stop the blaze from spreading, we moved in, and pulled out cases of slightly burnt sugar, butter and very warm tins of milk. The skin on our hands blistered with the heat

The women from The Garths lined up again, grateful for anything they could get, and we threw the cases out. One by one they walked the short distance home, up the concrete steps and into their flats to share their ill-gotten gains with their families.

And after the night in Fenwick's air raid shelter, Eastenders walked home after the all-clear had sounded, without a care in the world, singing and dancing in Coronation Street; the street that was forever the East End of Sunderland.

This was the East End of Sunderland in its time of greatest need. And within the confines of that small area, bordered by the River Wear, the town centre, and Hendon, could be found the type of community spirit, the sense of belonging and identity, that I have never found anywhere else in the world, despite my thousands of miles covered.

Despite our real poverty and hardship, rampant unemployment, our fathers and brothers serving in this bloody war, who may never come home again, ill-health, environmental pollution, basic accommodation, no money for hot water or heat, rationing and the very real threat of more bombs to come; despite all that, there was a real sense of community in the East End, a real and almost tangible collective camaraderie that could put a smile on a face where - if that face was elsewhere - it would only see endurance, gloom and despair.

The bombs kept coming, in rapid succession. The town's Victoria Hall – the scene of Sunderland's worst peace-time disaster when more than 180 children were crushed to death in a stampede in the 1880s – was hit by a parachute mine and the debris thrown into the air landed on the town's Winter Gardens in Mowbray Park, destroying what was Sunderland's answer to the Crystal Palace.

The town was among the country's top seven of most bombed towns and cities in the United Kingdom. The sirens put townsfolk on alert 247 times, the German air force dropped bombs on the town at least 35 times and 267 civilians were killed. Add to that the hundreds of Wearsiders killed in action, fighting for their country, and the hardship suffered by the people of the town, and only then can Wearside's contribution to the war effort be realised.

Perhaps it was that history, that sense of belonging, of camaraderie and of kinship and neighbourliness, and the feeling that I was always among friends, that always brought me home from my travels abroad. I have often been asked why I have never left Sunderland, when I could have gone elsewhere on the promise – more than a promise, really, almost a cast-iron certainty – that I would become a millionaire, and I have never been able to give a full and unequivocal answer. Perhaps the reason for that is, until now, I have never found the words.

The love I have for my hometown and its people have kept me there, still living in a council house, on a housing estate where my neighbours are often part of my audience, and where I feel comfortable. I could have made a fortune – many millions – if I had taken up any one of the many offers that have come my way over the years. But I chose not to take up those offers. I have met, and know, many millionaires whose lives are an empty shell, who count sycophantic arse-crawlers among their friends, for they have no true friends, and who believe success can be measured by their bank balance.

* * * * * * *

"Bobby!". I could hear the voice, but only vaguely.

"Bobby! Bobby!" I could hear the voice a little clearer, and feel the tug on my hospital-issue coverall, that covers your front but not your arse.

"How yer feeling, Bobby?"

It was my older brother Jonty, standing next to Diane, in the post-operative room, where I lay on a clammy bed, with so many wires and tubes leading from my orifices to machines it was difficult to fathom out where one started and another ended.

I could see Jonty and Diane, not clearly, more like two silhouettes. They were chatting to each other, but I couldn't hear what was being said, as a nurse busied herself checking monitors, heart rate, and the like.

"The boys all send their love," said Diane, as she stood nearer the bed. "Everyone's been ringing and asking how you are; people we've never heard from in years."

"You'll soon be back on your feet," said Jonty.

I wanted to say something, but the words wouldn't come. My whole body ached, and I felt so tired. My heavy eyelids fell and I was off again, into that comatose world that is somewhere between life and death.

Chapter Three

JIMMY WILLIES

"Go on, Jonty, go on, son," shouted my dad from the balcony outside the flat overlooking Coronation Street. "Give it some welly!"

Scores of neighbours stood on their own balconies whilst many others lined the street, their backs to the wall, as Jonty raced from the top of Coronation Street to the bottom bareback on a horse in what was one of the highlights of the week, the Sunday horse race.

The horses were provided by the likes of Tommy Bogie, the Greenwells, who ran a fruit and veg business, the Elliotts and the Padgetts. Some of the horses were used by tatters (hawkers or rag-and-bone men) during the week, or for deliveries, or for collecting coal or scrap metal washed up on the shores of Hendon Beach.

The race was a weekly spectacle and my brother Jonty was a regular rider, alongside Frankie Bogie, Tommy Clarke and his brother George.

Sometimes a few pounds would change hands in bets, but the race was more of a community event really; a bit of fun at the end of the week, to give the horses a bit of a run-out.

The race was always held after another regular weekly event, Sunday mass at St Patrick's Roman Catholic Church. The church was built for the many Irish people who came to live in the East End. Among the local Irish families was the Burkes, who ran a shop in Coronation Street.

A number of Italian families, specialising in the making and selling of delicious ice cream, also settled in the East End, among them were the Puccis, who had a shop in Coronation Street, the Ciarellas and the Valentes, who ran ice cream parlours in the East End and Hendon and, like their Irish counterparts, most were staunch Roman Catholic churchgoers.

Thomassey Pucci, one of the lads in the big Italian family, was a great friend of my brother Jonty and worked in the shop for many years until his dad closed it. He then got a job on a building site and died in a tragic accident after working on the buildings for only a few weeks.

My family wasn't devout Roman Catholic, but we did attend church, and the Roman Catholic influence was hard to avoid, what with us living in St Patrick's Garth and with me attending my first school, St Patrick's Roman Catholic Primary School, which was inside the garth and not even a stone's throw from the veranda outside our flat.

A teacher and one of the nuns visited our flat before I was accepted into the school and my mother put on a nice little spread, meat sandwiches and the like, but told me when I was asked if I wanted a meat sandwich I had to politely refuse, as there wasn't enough to go round and she wanted to impress our visitors. I did as she asked, turning down her offer of a tasty meat sandwich, and the teacher and the nun tucked in. What with all the rationing a meat sandwich was a bit of a treat. To my surprise, my mother then brought out a big bowl of peaches and a bowl of sweet-smelling custard, ready to dish out. I was absolutely bloody starving. "Would you like some peaches and custard?" My mother asked me. "I'd love some," I said. "Well, you can't have any," she said, "you wouldn't eat your meat!"

The teacher and the nun appeared to enjoy their food. They asked my mother if I had been baptised, if the family attended church every Sunday. They were impressed and I was accepted into the school

The teachers at St Pat's were mostly nuns who lived at the Sisters of Mercy Convent, attached to St Anthony's RC Grammar School for girls, in the Thornhill area of the town. The order of 50 or so nuns had been in Sunderland for many years and the sisters taught at all the catholic schools in the town. The first Sisters of Mercy – there was five of them - came over from Ireland in 1843 to establish the order.

St Pat's was renowned for its sense of order and discipline and religion was very much part of the school day, with prayer in morning assembly, sometimes the saying of the Holy Rosary, which meant repeating prayers over and over again, and the saying of the Catechism, which, again, meant repeating answers to questions asked by the nuns: "Do you reject Satan?", "I reject Satan."

There was always the same ritual every Monday morning when the nuns would line up all the kids on the hard stone floor in the main school building and ask each kid, one by one, if they had attended church the previous day. A straightforward "yes" was never acceptable to the nuns, they would ask which priest officiated and what the colour of his vestments were and how many altar boys helped out at the service. It was, of course, a sin to tell lies and a sin, in the nuns' eyes, not to attend church. If your lies were found out, then it was your duty to attend confession, where your sins would be absolved and you were given a clean slate. But your punishment was kneeling for half an hour on the hard stone floor in the corridor.

I could never fully understand the reasoning behind the absolute necessity of attending church every Sunday. No one could understand what the priest was saying anyway, as it was all in Latin.

Discipline at St Pat's was meted out in the form of the cane, a length of bamboo, and once hit your hand would be numb for hours. I wasn't exactly a willing pupil and I had a lot of trouble at St Pat's. When one of the nuns went to strike me with the cane, I ducked and it hit me on the eye, splitting the top of my eye right open. For my mother Meggie it was the final straw. She rushed over to the school, had a blazing row with the nun and took me out of the school. I was off school for several weeks until I underwent a sudden, religious conversion, from Roman Catholic to Protestant, and was enrolled at James William Street School, otherwise fondly known as Jimmy Willies.

It was at Jimmy Willies where some of my early friendships were forged; friendships that have lasted a lifetime, such as those with Tommy Reeves, Dickie Laws, Alan Milton and Ronnie Sweeney.

Jimmy Willies proved such a contrast to the harsh discipline and regimental routines of St Pat's and I began to enjoy my schooldays, running around the schoolyard, looking at the lasses doing PE with their skirts tucked into their navy blue knickers, knocking about with my mates and getting up to the usual stuff young lads get up to, like nicking lead from roofs.

The teachers at Jimmy Willies were great and some were real characters. A Mr Blossom always talked like W C Fields, calling the kids "my chick-a-dees". If discipline was needed he would jam a boy's head in the middle of the blackboard, trapping it guillotine-like, and give them six of the best with his ruler over their arse.

It was around this time I had my first taste of boxing, going three rounds with a lad from Glasgow in a local boys' club. He floored me within minutes and after I hit the canvas, the referee started his count. "What yer doing?" I asked. "I'm counting you out," said the ref. "Never mind that," I said. "I can count, call me a bloody ambulance."

*　*　*　*　*　*　*

I slowly opened my eyes and was almost blinded by the brightness of the hospital room. I hadn't eaten solids for what seemed to be days and my craving for a dose of nicotine was almost unbearable. After smoking 40 cigarettes a day for the best part of my adult life, it was hard to quit, just like that.

My eyes became accustomed to the light and in the corner of the room, sitting in an armchair, was my brother Charlie, reading a magazine.

"Giz a fag," I said.

"Oh, bloody hell, you must be getting better," said Charlie. "The first words you've uttered for days and it had to be those immortal words, 'giz a fag'."

"How long have you been sitting there?" I asked.

"About an hour. Diane had to nip home to see to the lads, so I said I'd keep an eye on you. I never realised you talked in your sleep."

"Really. What was I saying?" I asked.

"You were mumbling something; something about horses. I couldn't really understand what you were saying."

"It's funny," I said. "Lying here, not being able to do anything but think. I was remembering when we were lads down the garth and the races they use to have on a Sunday."

"Aye, there were good times," said Charlie. "We used to get up to all sorts of tricks. Can you remember going down to the cemetery at midnight, lying on one of the graves with a sheet over you, and scaring the shit out of everyone."

"That wasn't me. That was our Jonty," I said. "Anyway, what made you remember that?"

"Just looking at you lying there, with the sheet over you, looking like a ghost."

Walking through the cemetery in the East End, even during the day, was a bit of a challenge, as overhanging trees and large bushes made the place dark even on an afternoon. The cemetery, reputed to have been one of the stalking grounds of body-snatchers Burke and Hare, was eerie and frightening at night. As young lads it was considered a sign of manliness to walk through the cemetery at midnight.

Our Jonty once grabbed a white sheet from the house, walked into the cemetery and lay on a grave with the sheet over him. A few of us walked through the cemetery at midnight, as a bit of a dare and to show we had some bottle. When Jonty stood up and wailed like a banshee, we almost shit ourselves and darted off in all directions, most of us jumping over metal railings. Poor Tommy Barrass tried diving through a gap in the railings and got his head stuck firm. We had to call the fire brigade to free him.

"Do you think I'll ever walk again, Charlie?" I asked.

"Of course you will. You'll be back on stage before the end of the year."

Somehow, I didn't think so.

I knew the operation had been a success and I had the skilful surgeons at Sunderland General Hospital to thank for saving my life. But I was still as weak as a kitten, not even able to get up and go to the toilet, but having to lie in my own mess and rely on one of the hospital's team of dedicated nurses to clean up after me. I'd heard about how dedicated nurses are, but had never witnessed it first hand. No the wonder they call them angels.

Death, they say, is the great leveller but a close second must be illness serious enough to render you incapable of carrying out even the most basic of functions without someone's help. I was so grateful that the surgeons had given me a second chance and I was so grateful to the nurses for their care and devotion to duty.

But I couldn't see myself fit again. I couldn't imagine doing the everyday normal things we all take for granted and I couldn't see myself doing what I do best and what I enjoy – standing on stage, telling gags, and making people laugh.

As I lay in the intensive care unit I could only see myself being permanently disabled in some way. Despite the words of encouragement, which were welcome, and the positive attitude of all the staff, I did not believe that I would ever walk again. In fact, I did not believe that I would ever again stand up.

Chapter Four

THE BARROW BOYS

I was cleaning the fruit on the barrow on the bomb site in Union Street when this posh woman, the all fur-coat and no knickers type, approached the stallholder, my mate Dennis Cain.

"Can I help you, madam?" Asked Dennis.

"How much is a cucumber?" She asked.

"For you, madam, half a crown."

"How much is it for a half?" The woman asked.

"One shilling, tuppence halfpenny," said Dennis.

"How much for a quarter?"

"Sixpence, madam," said Dennis. "Only sixpence."

"Oh. I don't think I'll bother," said the woman turning to leave.

Dennis, a quick-witted individual full of patter, pushed the cucumber under her nose. "There you are madam," he said. "Have a sniff of my cucumber, completely free of charge."

The woman was as tight as a fish's arse, and often popped round to the bomb site just to catch up on the news. She was such a skinflint she wouldn't buy a newspaper.

It was an eye-opening experience, working the barrows, the wealthy people of the town counted every penny, and those who didn't have a pot to piss in bought most of the fruit and veg.

I started my working life as a barrow boy at the tender age of 14, having just left Jimmy Willies, without any qualifications to speak of and only a rudimentary grasp of the English language but a burning desire to get on. I didn't yet know what would help me get on, but I knew I would learn a lot with the barrow boys on the bomb site, where life was full of colour and character and the dawn of every new day brought with it a sense of adventure.

By this time I was living with the Clarke family. Jackie Clarke was big in the fruit and veg business; he had wagons and fruit stalls, and I worked alongside his sons, and my mates, Joe and his brothers Marky, John and Terry. There were other well-known East End names in the business; Richie Greenwell, one of the most generous men I had known who fed most of our veranda in the garths during the war, and his family, the Thorburns, the Chalks and the Longstaffs, to name but a few.

There had always been a thriving outdoor market in the East End. During the 1930s the market was situated between High Street East and Coronation Street and the early entrepreneurs there sowed the seeds for businesses that lasted for decades, among them William Chalk and Henry Chapman.

But with the East End slum clearance and after the town was bombed by the Nazis, the barrow boys' market also had to move, nearer to the town centre, on to the bomb site in Union Street, but that brought with it problems, as the site was owned by the council and the barrow boys were, technically, trespassers, without any right to be there.

As a barrow boy the day started early – at 4am – with the ten-mile drive to Newcastle in a wagon without lights (we left Sunderland at first light) to buy the fruit and vegetables, load them up, bring them back to the town, set up the stall, and start the working day.

And in Newcastle I mixed with and got to know some of the city's main characters who I would meet in later life; hard men with great stories to tell, like Bobby Snowdon, Panda Anderson, George "Blower" Shotton (who earned his name through his ability to blow safes), the Tamseys, Tommy the Fish, Mickey the Tash, Freddie the Beard, and Herbie Potter, who was always full of wisecracks.

I learned a lot listening to the barrow boys' quick-fire banter. Some of them were just natural comedians, great storytellers with impeccable timing, a kind of stage presence and a perfect delivery.

There was no sign, during any of our encounters, of this supposed intense rivalry between Newcastle and Sunderland; that only reared its ugly head at football matches with violent clashes between the brainless, dead-head, football hooligans who were, basically, soft as shite and only strong in numbers.

There was so much life on the bomb site, with people milling around looking for bargains to be had, the barrow boys touting for trade, lookouts keeping their eyes peeled for the old bill, punters arriving from all over the town and from the colliery towns and villages such as Seaham, Murton and the Trimdons. And every day there would be some kind of entertainment on the site, magicians, jugglers, buskers; one regular visitor was an escapologist who tied himself up, weighed himself down, and then the crowds would gather to see him free himself and throw halfpennies into his hat.

There was some money to be made on the barrows, but not a lot, and one of our main overheads was paying the fines imposed by the bench at Sunderland Magistrates' Court for trading on land without a licence or trespassing or obstruction or some other trumped-up charge.

Often the council would swoop on the bomb site to clear the barrow boys and the hawkers selling second-hand clothes, but we'd be back the next day and the crowds would be there to spend their few bob on apples, pears, bananas, strawberries and all the other fresh fruit and veg we'd picked up from Newcastle that morning.

One morning, in the spring of 1958, we arrived at the bomb site to find the council had stuck notices up everywhere informing us we had to quit the site, reminding us we were trespassers on council-owned land. We were given 12 hours to move all our gear.

So we packed our stuff and moved on to another bomb site in Brougham Street, where we stayed until the early summer, only to be issued with another ultimatum from the council to quit the site.

It was rough justice really. It wasn't as if the site was going to be used for anything else. The barrow boys and the hawkers were just ordinary people trying to make a few bob, not doing anyone any harm, but the council saw us as a nuisance. If money was crap the same type of officials would probably issue notices demanding we sew up our arseholes.

If, for whatever reason, we couldn't work on the barrows, then we'd be out with the horse and cart tatting – or hawking – collecting rags and woollens to be weighed-in for cash, collecting scrap metal, or coal dust washed up at Hendon from the colliery spoil heaps further down the coast.

One local character, Albie Thompson, used to walk from the East End to Hendon Beach virtually every day, pushing a big pram in which he would load scrap metal which had been washed up. Some people wondered why the hell he did it – believing there couldn't be much cash in it. Albie Thompson built up a building empire and became a millionaire.

One of the most well-known tatters in the East End was Bull Rennie; that's all he did all his life. My uncle Tommy Dobbin was one of the tatters and me and my mate little Ronnie Sweeney often went out with him collecting rags and woollens. Once we were out in Ryhope on a hot summer's day and I asked a resident for a glass of water, to which she duly obliged. Then I asked her if she had a drink for Dobbin, and she told me there was a pail of water in the outhouse. My Uncle Tommy was a bit of a workhorse, but he wasn't a horse.

When little Ronnie Sweeney accompanied me on the tatting trips we were guaranteed quite a big pay-out, not because he was better than anyone else at collecting rags and woollens, it was because I would hide him in the pile and weigh him in as part of the load of rags. We got away with that a few times before the scrap yard boss cottoned on.

From the age of 14, when I left school, through my early teenage years living with my Uncle Jackie Clarke – a big man in the town – my life was the barrows, tatting, collecting coal and sometimes manure, seeing the family, ducking and diving, bobbing and weaving, making a few bob where I could.

Often there would be ten of us lads sleeping in a room in the Clarke's house, all bollock-naked, boasting about our latest, often imaginary, sexual conquests. There was the Young brothers, the Storeys, the Reeves, Tommy and Ronnie Miller, Ronnie Sweeney, Jackie Clarke's sons – all great pals of mine, and life was a barrel of laughs.

We'd spend some of our hard-earned cash in the Crown Billiard Hall in Fawcett Street, watching some of the East End hard men playing snooker or just having a bit crack on. Some of the best streetfighters in the town got in the Crown and we, the younger generation, were in awe of them. One of them was Eugene Derry, one of the toughest fighters in the town, who commanded a great deal of respect. Then there was Ernie Bewick, Charlie McDonald (Chucky Mack), Michael Wharton, who was later done for manslaughter, Jack Casey, who did most of his fighting in the ring and became a great champion, and a man who I saw in action a few times and who I considered the hardest fighter in Sunderland, Jimmy Nairns.

These were men who did not go looking for a fight, but fights would often come their way because of their reputations. They were all respected, feared and fearless. This was the environment in which I grew up and, at an impressionable age, learned some of life's early lessons, like survival. It toughened me up.

One of the most entertaining annual get-togethers in the East End was the carnival down on the Town Moor, which attracted visitors from across the North East and a wide range of entertainers, some with the most bizarre acts imaginable.

There was a fella with one leg who would climb a ladder and dive into a pool of water only about two feet deep. Strongmen would lift twice their weight, escapologists would tie themselves up in knots, and local fighters would take to the ring to see if they could go three rounds with a tough, talented, boxer.

The pie eating contest was always popular and a big young lad called George Craig, who sometimes helped me on the barrows, entered, scoffed 12 pies and won the cash.

I walked home with young George after the carnival and he was still wiping the gravy from his mouth.

"Please don't tell me ma I won the pie eating contest," he pleaded.

"Why the hell not?" I asked.

"Because I'll not get any supper," said young George.

* * * * * * *

I woke up laughing. It had been a long time since I laughed. There didn't seem to be much to laugh about, still in a lot of pain, still nil by mouth, still lying in bed, with nothing to do but think, reminisce, take stock, and wonder how long I had left to think and look back. Nostalgia, a thing of the past, was keeping my mind alert while my body slowly worked to heal the scars left by the seven-hour operation to fit a lengthy tube inside me and defeat the aneurysm that had so nearly claimed my

41

life. I was trying to be positive, trying to fight back, but, if there was light somewhere at the end of this tunnel, it seemed I was still waiting to enter the tunnel. The doctors had told me it would take time and I had to learn to be patient, but words of comfort and reassurance failed to diminish the sheer frustration of it all.

"Would you like a grape?"

Richie Greenwell had sold millions of grapes, most fed to patients in hospital getting over operations like me. Why was it always grapes?

"Hello Richie," I said. "Have you come for that thirty five quid I still owe you?"

Richie laughed: "Well, as that happened more than 50 years ago, that thirty five quid will be worth, what, about two and a half grand now, with interest?"

My old employer had a good memory. I never had returned that day's takings from the barrows when all I sold all day was strawberries, pounds and pounds of strawberries.

Like most teenagers I was rather impetuous, a little hot-headed, did things on the spur of the moment without thinking about the consequences. That day I pocketed the thirty five quid, packed my gear, ran down to the town's railway station, and hopped on a train to London. What I hoped to find there, in the bright lights of the capital paved with gold, I don't really know. I saw a few of the sights, slept rough for a couple of nights, then returned home on the train, penniless and fearing the wrath of Richie Greenwell. I expected at least a good hiding from him, or from one of the older barrow boys. But it never came.

"How yer feeling, Bobby?" Asked Richie.

"Why man I'm top of the bill," I said. "On the mend. The staff in here are bloody marvellous."

The nurse, my nurse, smiled.

"All the lads have been asking after you," said Richie. "The Clarke's, the Thorburn lads, even some of the lads from Newcastle."

"That's kind of them," I said. "You know people's been ringing Diane up at home, saying how sorry they are at hearing the news."

"What the news that you're ill?" Asked Richie.

"No," I said. "The news that I'm bloody dead. It's funny how these things spread. It's a wonder our lass hasn't had a visit from Duckworth's."

I grabbed a grape from the bag, but before I could pop it into my gob, the eyes of the nurse were on me like a hawk.

"All right, all right," I said. "I get the message. I suppose that also mean's a cigarette's out of the question?"

Chapter Five

THE ROCK N' ROLL BOYS

The suit was immaculate, cut to perfection, fitted where it touched and when I looked at the full-length mirror in Jackson the Tailor's shop in Sunderland I felt like a million dollars.

"There's just one problem," I told the tailor.

"What's that then?"

"You can see my bollocks."

The problem of exposed bollocks was soon solved by me wearing a pair of thick white underpants and when I took to the stage that night in the Norfolk Hotel the suit caused a sensation. I'd got the idea for a white suit from a film I had seen in one of the local cinemas, if I remember rightly the movie was simply called The Man in the White Suit. It made me stand out from the crowd. No one in Sunderland had ever worn a white suit, it just wasn't practical, and some of the poor blokes didn't even own a suit of any description.

As I belted out the Everly Brothers' hit, Wake Up Little Suzie, the current number one record in the charts, I was in my element and the crowd supping their drinks and singing along were loving every minute of it.

After the sharp finish to the song, I had the audience in the palm of my hand. I'd made a connection.

"I was stopped by the cops in Fawcett Street the other day," I said.

"I wound the window down and the cop asked 'what's your name?'

"'Knoxall,' I said. 'Where yer from?' 'Blackhall,' I said. 'What's this car you're driving.' 'Vauxhall', I said. 'What's in the boot?' 'F, f, find out for yourself, officer'."

The crowd erupted, and I was enjoying myself. A young, blonde, fit barmaid passed, collecting empty beer glasses.

"Hello love," I said. "Bye, you're a beautiful young woman." The barmaid looked slightly embarrassed. "Don't be shy," I said. "Just tell me one thing. What is it that turns on a gorgeous young woman like you?"

"Cowboys and Jewish men," she said.

The crowd roared. "What's yer name, love?" I asked.

"Denise," she said, "what's yours?"

"Hopalong Cohen."

It was 1957 and the awesome sound of Rock n' Roll had arrived in Sunderland, over the pond they call the Atlantic, and the town was buzzing with great music, flash cars, all the big Hollywood movies showing at the local cinemas, sharp suits and, after the post-war depression, people appeared to have cash in their pockets.

For local women many things were on the up; hair and hemlines among them, and for the young Bobby Knoxall and his mates Dickie Laws, Jackie Clarke, Alan Milton, Ronnie Sweeney and Jackie Longstaff, opportunity was banging loudly at our doors.

It all started a couple of years earlier, really, when I was introduced to the world of the boozer and drink. Boozers I liked, and there were scores of them in the East End of Sunderland and in the town centre, and they were full of local characters. Beer, I didn't like. I drank no more than two pints of beer on my first night out and puked all the way home. I never drank beer again. But I met Ron, who became a lifelong friend. His full name was Ron Bacardi and he was always accompanied by his best mate, coke.

After a hard week on the barrows we barrow boys, despite most of us being under-age, would end up in any one of a number of pubs, The Central, The Three Crowns, Polly's Bar, The Bridge Hotel, The Norfolk Hotel or The Bells, where Mrs Brown played the piano and her husband Jackie played the drums, or in a pub run by Big Raymond, a tall, handsome, gay guy who was the toughest queer in the town.

In many of the pubs people would start a drunken singalong and in most one of the highlights of the night was a scrap, a toe-to-toe barney, where two local hard men would beat seven bells out of each other. I witnessed a hell of a lot of fights.

I collected glasses in some of the pubs, then started to sing a couple of songs. Soon the manager of the Norfolk Hotel was asking me to take command of the place on a Tuesday and Thursday night, singing a few songs myself and arranging for other entertainers to take to the stage. The nights proved a big hit.

Then Dickie Laws suggested we formed a band. Many of the popular hits coming out of America, and Britain, were easy to play. Dickie, whose father was big in the tyre business and was quite wealthy, had a decent singing voice, as did Alan Milton, who also played double bass, and little Ronnie Sweeney had taught himself to play a decent tune on the saxaphone. Our band, The Rock n' Roll Boys, was born.

We didn't have a regular drummer and our group was extremely raw, but we were learning fast. One of our first gigs, where we earned about two pounds each for the night, was at a workingmen's club in Sacriston, County Durham. The hostile crowd booed us off stage – they obviously had no taste or were still too much into mid 1950s ballads – there was a hell of a fight and the police were called. We didn't return to Sacriston for several years.

Our big break in our hometown came at the Pallion Workingmen's Club which, at the time, was doing booming business. The crowd liked us so much we were re-booked almost immediately.

Then other bookings came in thick and fast, many at the old colliery towns and villages in County Durham; Seaham, Murton, Easington, Peterlee, Blackhall, Ryhope, and at the ages of 15 and 16 we were earning ourselves a bit of a reputation.

Jackie Longstaff, who used the stage-name Johnny, had the best singing voice I had ever heard and could compete with the best of them. He did a fantastic impression of Johnny Ray, but didn't need to sing under the shadow of anyone else, he could hold his own on any stage in the country.

Jackie, the son of a Murton miner, who became a lifelong friend, started singing at the tender age of 13 in the school yard at Murton Secondary Modern. He sang at a few local clubs, such as that in South Hetton, but had to leave at 9.30pm, with him being only 13. He did a few shows with that famous North East comedian Bobby Thompson, "The Little Waster".

Jackie's big break came when he won the regional heat of the Carol Levis Discoveries Talent Show, signing Drink To Me Only With Thine Eyes. The national final was due to be staged at the Royal Albert Hall, but difficulties with sound meant it had to be transferred to a theatre in Villiers Street, from where they produced the Carol Levis Radio Show. In the final Jackie came a close second to a young contralto with a voice like an angel who made it big in opera. Carrots MacMichael, the young lass was called, on account of her bright red hair. If I remember rightly her real first name was Marjorie. Jackie went on a three-month tour with the other Discoveries playing in Liverpool, Glasgow, Cardiff, Sheffield, Leeds and other major towns and cities.

The Rock n' Rolls Boys were playing in the Norfolk Hotel on a night when Jackie was also singing. I was impressed with his voice and asked him to join our band. It was the start of a partnership, and a friendship, that kept us both in show-business, earning a decent living, for more than 50 years.

In the beginning there were no agents, the 15 and ten per-centers came along a little later, and Jackie would handle the club concert stewards and take our bookings.

The comedy crept into the act gradually, really, and, for me, it took over. I'd sing the Rock n' Roll songs, Alan Milton would sing a few numbers, and Jackie Longstaff would belt out a few ballads. In between songs I'd crack a gag a night, then it became two or three gags a night, then nine or ten. I could do this, I thought, and in the pubs and clubs of Sunderland and County Durham I slowly graduated from singer to comedian. I had found something that I was very good at, and something which the audiences loved. From there my act developed, becoming more visual, with me performing acrobatics on stage, wriggling out of my jacket when bursting into a Rock n' Roll hit, gesturing, posing, gesticulating, contorting my body like a man made of rubber, twisting my face this way and that and perfecting the mannerisms and body language that became the Knoxall trademark. This was more than stand-up comedy. I used every muscle in my body to express myself, and the crowds loved it. I had just started out on my career in comedy and I was already, sometimes quite literally, flying.

What I didn't know then, and what I couldn't even have visualised, was that the talent I had would take me all over the globe, to some of the world's most exotic, sun-drenched, picture-postcard, locations, and that I would meet Royalty, Prime Ministers, gangsters, famous footballers and boxers, some of the biggest names in Hollywood, and work alongside some of the world's greatest stars.

*   *   *   *   *   *   *

The nurse ripped the thick bandage from my guts and the pain was indescribable. It had only been a few days since the operation but the scar had, surprisingly, healed quite well. I had been moved from the intensive care unit to a room adjoining one of the general wards and it was great to see people again; people who knew me from my stage act and my close friends from the East End and elsewhere.

The get-well-soon cards had come in from all over the world and the telephone was hot with people asking me how I was getting on, when I would be out, on my feet again, and back home on stage.

"Do you want to try and sit in the chair?" Asked Diane, who was in the room with her sister Vicky, who had travelled up from her home in Rochester, Kent, and my sister Violet. Diane, Violet and Vicky had been absolute bricks during my gamble with death, absolute pillars of strength. Our four boys had been worried sick and it must have been difficult balancing visits to the hospital with running a home and working.

"I don't think I can move, Diane," I said. "I'm finding it difficult just to sit up in bed."

"Well. As long as you're comfortable," she said. "We all know you'll be back on your feet in no time."

I would soon be starting physiotherapy, which would help, but my fight back to fitness wasn't going to come overnight. I could always fight – I was Sunderland's first kickboxing streetfighter, as I preferred using my feet to my fists – but the road to my recovery was proving to be one hell of a fight.

MEET THE PARENTS

Clockwise (from top). My dad, John Thomas McKenna and he and my mother Meggie Annie, on their wedding day. Gran McKenna, Annie Kelly (a formidable woman). Diane's mother Minnie and her father Bill.

EARLY DAYS IN THE EAST END

Top: Mam, dad, my sister, Kim and niece Karen in St Pat's Garth, in the East End of Sunderland.

Right: My big brother Jonty (on left) with Thomassey Pucci (right), Billy Kerr and two lady friends.

THE STUNNER

My beautiful wife Diane as a young model (right) and (below) later with a friend.

OLD FRIENDS

Dickie Laws (below left) and Tom Bogie, one of my first agents.

BARROW BOYS

One of my first publicity shots (left) and (below) a very rare, and faded, photograph of the barrow boys on the bomb site in Sunderland town centre.

A FEW SCRAPS

Top: Hoping to fly to The Falklands to entertain our lads.

Below: In Gordon Souter's scrap yard in Seaham, which I opened.

THE ROCK N ROLL BOYS

Left: Starting off in showbusiness.

Below: With my new white suit, rocking it up in the Norfolk Hotel, Sunderland.

A FEW CHARACTERS

Top left: Eddie Britton, a bouncer at Wetherells night-club and one of Sunderland's first licensed private detectives.

Top right: Me at The Pallion Club.

Left: Old school pal John King (at left) and (at right) Big Raymond, licensee of many pubs and the hardest homosexual to have lived in Sunderland.

GANGLAND CONNECTIONS

Left: In conversation with the London underworld mediator and my former boss and friend Peter Hubbard.

Bottom left: Playboy and convicted killer Dennis Stafford, who was a business associate of my former boss, the King of the North East bandit empire, Vince Landa (below).

Chapter Six

PRIVATE KNOXALL

The piercing eyes of the sergeant stared straight into mine and, despite the fact he had only just met me, his eyes, for some reason, were full of hatred. He was a typical Army sergeant, devoted to his duty, with a loud mouth, immaculate kit, highly-polished boots and the type of walk that made you think he had a poker up his arse. He was a sergeant with the Durham Light Infantry (Second Battalion) and I was a raw recruit, standing to attention on the first day of my six-weeks Army training at the training camp at Brancepeth, near Durham City. From getting my call-up papers I knew the Army wasn't for me but, for two years, whether I liked it or not, I had my time to serve for Queen and country.

"Are you fit, lad? The sergeant asked bellowing down my ear-hole.

"I'm reasonably fit," I said.

"Done a bit of boxing, have you?" He asked.

"I've had a few rounds," I replied.

"Right then. You can go a few rounds with me."

The bout was set for later in my first week in the Army in the gym, but, apparently, there would be no one else there, just me and the sergeant. It seemed very strange but, I thought, maybe this was part of the Army induction process, to test how hard you were, to see if you were up to the exacting demands of Army life.

I'd heard quite a lot about the Army, from my brother Jonty, who was coming to the end of his National Service after being out in Germany and Malaya and some other far-flung countries. He knew the score, he was Army savvy, and he made a good soldier. A better soldier than I would ever make.

Why the sergeant had taken an instant dislike to me, I didn't know. Maybe it was because standing there in my civvies, long coat, trilby hat, sharp suit and suede shoes, I represented everything he did not. I looked like a spiv, because I was a spiv and he, probably, thought of himself as an officer and a gentleman.

The lads I joined up with were great, we had some good laughs, but Army life wasn't suiting me at all. I couldn't wear Army regulation boots, because I'd never worn hard boots, they just chaffed away at the skin on my feet. I couldn't wear an Army tunic, because I came out in a hell of a rash, and I couldn't even wear an Army peaked cap, because it rested on a relatively new scar on my forehead, picked up during a barney at a nightclub in Sunderland. All the signs were there for officers to realise that Army life and me were not compatible. As I couldn't wear the full Army uniform, I couldn't go on parade, and would be given other tasks to do while the rest of the lads did their square-bashing. It didn't make them resentful towards me. I'm sure many thought I was pulling the wool over the officers' eyes, but I wasn't. I had real problems with the Army kit. I also had problems with discipline. I didn't like jumped-up little Hitlers barking their orders down my ear-hole. I sometimes reacted, and ended up in the slammer.

There were a few funny incidents I heard about while the lads were on parade. One morning they were all lined up and the sergeant stared at one of the rookie soldiers and asked what his problem was. "I've got piles," he said. "You've got piles?" Said the sergeant. "Don't you want to be a good soldier?" "Yes," said the private. "Then get yourself into the washhouse early, get the wire brush, and scrub those piles!"

The sergeant moved along the parade line and saw another rookie looking dodgy. "What's your problem, soldier?" He asked. "I've got mouth ulcers," said the private. "Then get yourself round to the wash-house early in the morning, get the wire brush, and brush those ulcers away." "I will, sergeant," said the private. "Don't you want to be a good soldier?" The sergeant asked. "No," said the rookie. "I just want to get round to the wash-house and get the wire brush before he does."

One of my old mates from the East End was determined to get out of his National Service, saying he could not be expected to join-up, as he had one leg shorter than the other. "Don't you worry about that," the medical officer told him. "The ground won't be level where you'll be fighting."

A few days passed and the night of my boxing bout with the sergeant came around. He was a tough fighter, he actually boxed for the Army, and he hit me so hard, I thought I was surrounded. The sergeant almost killed me and I was taken to the billet with blood gushing from a deep cut in my eye. He had re-opened the old nightclub wound that had prevented me from wearing a peaked Army cap.

My brother Jonty had just returned from Germany that day and when he came to see me in the billet, he was bloody furious. He asked me who had done it. I just told him I was beaten fair and square by the sergeant in the boxing ring.

That weekend, on weekend leave, unusually, Jonty went into Durham City for a night out. The sergeant happened to be enjoying a night out in the same area. Jonty had a great night. The sergeant ended up in hospital, bloodied, bruised and bewildered.

It was only later that I discovered why the sergeant had taken an instant dislike to me. When Jonty had first started his National Service at Brancepeth the same sergeant had asked him if he was fit and challenged him to a boxing bout. Unlike me, Jonty came off best. He bloody flattened him. The sergeant had held a grudge ever since.

After our six weeks' initial training at Brancepeth, we did further training at the Deerbolt Centre near Barnard Castle, County Durham, and were flown out to be stationed in Wuppertal, Germany. It was my first experience of life abroad, but it really wasn't like life abroad, it was life in an Army camp that was Wuppertal's Little England.

I dreamt about and thought about my hometown, our little band, the Rock n' Roll Boys, the work I could be doing in the clubs, working on the barrows with the others lads, and the tatters, and everything else that summed up my early life in Sunderland's East End. Like most of the rookie soldiers I got homesick. Most didn't do anything about it, just got on with their lives as best they could. But me, I went absent without leave, AWOL on one of my first weekends back home. I decided I didn't want to go back.

It wasn't long before the Military Police sent an escort to Sunderland to take me back to Wuppertal. The escort was my old mate Stevie "Sausage" New, who I knocked about with as a kid and who came from a large East End family.

Stevie was nicknamed "Sausage" because he had inherited the name from his dad and his dad had been given the label because he used to keep two pigs in a room at the family home in Nile Street. He would never be without sausage, ran the joke, and the name stuck. It was the same for "Monkey" Oliver, another of the original East End barrow boys. The name had been passed down from father to son and the father had earned the nick-name because of his amazing ability to climb the scaffolding and gantries in the Sunderland shipyards, without any ropes or harnesses, just like a monkey flying through the jungle, hopping from tree to tree. One of the tatters was simply called Conky and few of us, including myself, ever used his real name. In fact, I sadly can't remember what his real name was. Conky was only given the name because he had a large nose – a large "conk". It was strange, but he went through life being called Conky on account of his large nose, and never raised any objections.

Stevie "Sausage" New, when he came to escort me back to Germany, said he had to put the hand-cuffs on me. I told him if that's what he had to do, that's what he had to do. I was taken to Gill Bridge Police Station to be held there while the papers and my travel details were sorted out and, when the day arrived for my escort to accompany me on the train south to the Army base from where we would be flown back out to Germany, I asked Sausage if he'd allow me to nip to my mother's house in St Pat's Garth for a quick freshen-up and a change of clothes, he said there was no problem.

On arriving at the north end of Sunderland Railway Station me and Sausage ended up in The Three Crowns for a quick drink before our journey south. One drink became two, then three, then four, and Sausage decided he wasn't going back, either. We spent the next few days tatting, or on the barrows, much as we had done before National Service, then the Military Police were sent for us again. It was probably the one and only time in Sunderland that an Army escort had to be sent to the town to collect an Army escort, and the soldier he was meant to be escorting, to escort them both back to the Army Camp.

Private Knoxall – I had earned my nickname because of the number of people I used to knock about at Jimmy Willies School – could still not settle into Army life and the straw that broke the camel's back, for which I was discharged from the Army with ignominy, came during one heavy-drinking, heavy-brawling, wet weekend in Wuppertal when myself, a mate from Hartlepool called Ali Sharpe, and another couple of squaddies, decided to paint the town red and show some local German folk what exactly was meant by Sunderland East End hospitality. For one German it meant hospital.

A few weeks before our weekend of debauchery a fellow English squaddie called Percival had been stabbed in Wuppertal and bled to death. Naturally, there was tension in the air when English soldiers were out for a good time and the local German hostility towards us was reciprocated. When the battle commenced it was World War II all over again, bars were trashed, fists, feet and beer glasses and bottles flew and one local German bloke ended up in hospital with a serious eye injury after a bloody battle spilled out into the street.

Back in our billet we slept off our hangovers, none the worst for the ordeal, but the following morning, bright and early, the Military Police marched in with a German man and he pointed to me, my mate Ali Sharpe and another squaddie called Johnson.

We were marched off, put into solitary and later court-martialled for affray. We were each sentenced to 18 months jail and spent nine months in total in a local German prison. After my sentence I was returned to Brancepeth and discharged with ignominy, in other words for the disgraceful act which led to the court martial for affray. I should have returned home from the Army in disgrace, but I didn't. I just felt relieved that the whole bloody ordeal was over with and I could get on with my life without any trumped-up, loud-mouthed, stripe-shouldered arsehole barking orders and expecting me to jump.

I thought that would have been my last tour of duty with service personnel, but shortly after my return home to the local workingmen's clubs circuit, I was called up for action abroad again. But this time I would be barking the orders and telling the gags, on stage entertaining American troops. It was to be my first taste of working as a comedian in a foreign country and it gave me a new lease of life and a taste for adventure and international travel.

* * * * * * *

It was my tenth cup of tea and it wasn't even yet midday. I seemed to be surviving on nothing more than tea and lemonade, gallons and gallons of the stuff. If the nurses had decided to put two drips by my bedside, one full of tea the other lemonade, I wouldn't have got any exercise at all those first few days. Lifting a cup to my lips was my only exercise, hardly strenuous, but at least it was some kind of activity. It was an activity I was thankful for. If things had not gone my way I wouldn't be here at all, enjoying a cup of tea.

"Ah. The simple pleasures in life," I said.

"But I bet you wish that was Bacardi," said Ronnie Sweeney, on one of his regular visits.

"You know, Ronnie," I said. "I couldn't give a fuck if I never drink Bacardi again. I probably kept the company going for nigh on 40 years."

Ronnie laughed.

"Why is it that you never drank beer, like us normal blokes?" Ronnie asked.

"Because I couldn't keep the bugger down." I said. "My first taste of beer was my last."

"What's been happening in the world then, Ronnie?" I asked.

"Just the usual," he said. "Plenty of fights down the city centre, a few muggings and Peter Reid insisting that the team performed well getting beat 4-0 at Chelsea at the weekend."

"Who the hell's he trying to kid?" I asked. "This is the worst season we've had for years. Wouldn't be surprised if we go down."

"If they don't win on Saturday," said Ronnie, "we'll be in the bottom three. It'll be a bloody struggle getting back from that."

"Peter Reid was on the blower the other day asking how I was," I said. "Loads of the lads have been on and some have sent cards, big Niall Quinn, Mickey Gray, Kevin Ball."

"Didn't you used to go into the dressing room before a match and tell a few gags to boost the lads before kick-off?" Asked Ronnie.

"Aye. All the time," I said.

"Maybe that's why we heading for relegation," Ronnie joked.

"You cheeky little bastard," I said. "If I could get out of this bed, I'd knock you out the fucking window."

I'd been associated with Sunderland Football Club for more than 40 years and hardly missed a home match, when I was home. Some of the old school, like Charlie Hurley, had gone into after-dinner speaking and I'd arrange the shows, act as the Master of Ceremonies, telling gags and introducing the speakers.

It was nice that many of the Sunderland players old and new had been asking after me after my operation, including the under-pressure manager Peter Reid, whom I got on very well with.

It was just a pity I wasn't fit enough to get down to the stadium and gee the lads up a bit before a match. Or, perhaps, it was just as well I wasn't there, as Ronnie had so eloquently quipped, because I wouldn't like to think I had a part to play in this great club's downfall.

As I lay in my hospital bed, I'm sure many of the first team players felt exactly the way I did – bloody useless.

Chapter Seven

THE GRASSY KNOLL

The assassination of President John F Kennedy brought a great nation to its knees in shock, disbelief, anger and soul-searching. It also brought English comedian Bobby Knoxall a great deal of distress and anxiety, because I couldn't earn any money.

Back home in Sunderland the nightclub scene was really taking off with Wetherells, which had been officially opened by recording star Ronnie Hilton earlier in the year, The Odeon, the Empire Theatre and Seaburn Hall, which had just undergone a £45,000 refurbishment, packing them in by attracting the top acts of the day. A buzzing new nightclub, the La Strada, had also just opened its doors.

The Beatles, Helen Shapiro, Gene Vincent, Billy Fury, Joe Brown, The Tornados, Danny Williams, Karl Denver, Del Shannon, The Bachelors and Cilla Black were just a few of the acts that had topped the bill in my home town in the weeks leading up to my departure from England, to tour Germany and later Naples, Tripoli and Turkey, entertaining the soldiers, sailors and airmen and women of the United States' Army, Navy and Air Force.

I ended up touring and entertaining the American troops after agents from the United States visited clubs in North East England talent-spotting. They liked my act and I was signed up to an American/German Artistes' Agency run by a chap called Charlie Clop. I was flown over to Germany on a three-month contract with the promise of more work to come if things worked out, which I hoped they would.

The first three months were spent in Germany, touring all the US bases, and I had never come across such a mixed audience. Canadians, Texans, New Yorkers, Californians, blacks, whites, Mexicans, Chinese, Puerto Ricans, native American Indians. It was one hell of a challenge connecting with such a wide-ranging audience. The biggest challenge was getting the crowd to laugh and the other big challenge was not upsetting anyone; otherwise there could have been riots.

I did three shows a night, the officers' clubs, the enlisted men's clubs, working alongside one of America's top singing stars Brooke Benton, girl singers and speciality acts; it was a full show.

In Turkey I teamed up with a clever lad called Rennie Lawford, one of the top officers in the Royal Navy, from London, who was working on the entertainment side. One night we got pissed out of our brains and Rennie challenged me to ride a camel. I told him that was no problem, as I'd ridden horses bareback as a lad in Coronation Street. I mounted the camel legless, bobbed up and down a bit, then got thrown off. The police were called and Rennie, being a bit of a joker, warned the cops that I was a Dillinger, gangster-type, who carries a gun. They rushed me into a cockroach-infested cell in a police station, stripped me naked and searched me. The British consulate was called and what could have been a diplomatic crisis was over before it had even begun. I wasn't charged with anything.

We were flown out to Naples for a tour of the US bases but, even before the tour got underway, news quickly spread of Kennedy's assassination in Dallas. The assassin, I heard, pulled the trigger when he was standing either on or near a grassy knoll. That grassy knoll featured a lot in the enquiry that followed.

The shocking news changed the whole mood of the place, and all the entertainment was cancelled. No one was in the mood for signing, dancing and listening to gags. Rennie and I were stuck in the hotel in Naples, constantly on the phone to our agent to find us work, but there was no work, and we were skint. I had to phone home asking my family if they had any cash to send over but, of course, they were all struggling to make ends meet as it was.

Then Rennie, who was a clever lad, came up with an idea. He had seen a photograph in one of the hotels of a flying ace known as Captain Jack, who, for whatever reason, was associated with the hotel. Perhaps he had stayed there, I don't know. Rennie and I visited the hotel and, over a drink, he remarked, en passant: "Oh. I see you have a photograph of Captain Jack on the wall."

"Oh. You know him?" The manager behind the bar asked.

"A very good friend of mine," said Rennie. "We go back a lot of years."

The hotel manager was very impressed and, after hearing we were in show-business with no work on because of the Kennedy assassination, he invited us to perform in his hotel. Rennie's cunning ploy had worked. We both went to the beach, inviting all the Brits to the hotel that night, and we packed it out. Rennie was a fantastic tenor singer, doing all the top opera songs, and I gave the crowd a comic taste of home.

After Naples we drove to Visbaden to get our money owed from Charlie Clop, then drove on to the Hook of Holland, where we secured a passage to England on a boat. Rennie just left the car there, there was nothing else he could do and when we arrived in Dover he got one of his brothers from London to pick us up and we stayed in the capital for a couple of days.

Rennie ended up travelling with me to the North East and stayed with my mother and the family for a few days. We went to see a few agents, Doris and Tommy Bogie and Ronnie Prenelle, and we played a few of the local clubs together, along with my old friend Jackie Longstaff. Rennie later got an agent of his own and he settled in the North East, marrying a girl from South Shields.

My tour of Germany entertaining the troops had made the newspapers in my hometown, thanks in no small way to a man who became my unofficial Press agent, Len Harper, a man with a huge intellect who became a very good friend of mine. Len had only just been elected to the town council. Born in Southwick, Sunderland, Len was a very educated man who studied at the town's Bede Grammar School then went on to higher education at Durham University before joining the Royal Navy where he attained the rank of Lieutenant. Len was a shrewd politician and would later rise through the ranks to become the Leader of Sunderland Borough Council and the town's Mayor. He also played a major part in breathing new life into the town's Empire Theatre, where, at the age of 14, I would watch classic entertainers such as Frank Randall. Len suggested that I could become an ambassador for my hometown on my foreign travels, sending something back to Sunderland from wherever I was, and his connections with the local newspaper, The Sunderland Echo, kept my profile high, even when I was thousands of miles away from home.

On my return to Sunderland it was obvious that the nightlife and club scene were taking off in a big way. Wetherells and La Strada were doing a roaring trade and it was only a few months before yet another new nightspot, The Blue Note, in Roker Avenue, opened its doors to the public. Bob Monkhouse and Gerry Dorsey (who later changed his name to Engelbert Humperdinck) were among the stars to top the bill at Wetherells and business was also booming at The Empire Theatre and at Seaburn Hall.

Out of all the nightclubs in the town there was one that became a magnet for the stars themselves who would be able to wind down after a show, or visit on a night off. The club was the Ro Ko-Ko, which was on the seafront at Roker, and it attracted a Bohemian crowd, artistes, gangsters, wide-boys, agents, even members of the local Press corps. The club was conventional in some ways, such as the house rule that all male visitors had to wear a tie. The comic Spike Milligan fell foul of that rule one night and was refused entry.

In the early to mid 1960s the North East was being flooded with stars who, relatively unknown then on the national scene, would make it big; Freddie Starr, The Delmont's, Tony Christie, Frank Carson, Dustin Gee, Johnny Duffy, Dukes and Lee. Johnny Duffy, a great singer whom I later worked with, had his own minder, Mitzy Walsh, who brought him up to the North East. Mitzy was a big name in Blackpool, running the doors.

The Ro Ko-Ko was the in place for entertainers in Sunderland and it had a fantastic atmosphere. Most of the entertainers appearing locally would meet up there at about 10pm, exchange a few stories, get up on the stage for ten minutes or so and have a laugh until closing time. Many deals were done there, booking acts for the nightclubs or the working-men's clubs. Jack Atkinson and Bill Tait were two of its early managers, both great characters.

Despite my reputation as a streetfighter who used his feet better than he could use his fists, I got into hundreds of scraps at the Ro Ko-Ko. A visiting American, only about 6ft 8ins tall, decided to chance his arm and landed me such a heavy punch I went flying through a window, fell 20ft and ripped my right hand open. There was blood everywhere. I went to the hospital to get stitched up, but returned later and, as the American fella was so big, I armed myself with a hammer. I hit him with it, and he got back up. I hit him twice, and he did not get back up. An ambulance was called and he ended up in hospital.

One night four Swedish bodybuilders started working themselves in the club and, with the help of my mate George Craig, we floored the lot of them.

The Ro Ko-Ko was all booze, birds, laughs, fights, gambling and show-business. One particularly drunken night myself and a few other regulars had a wager on who could swim from the north pier to the south pier the quickest. It was a bloody freezing early morning when we raced into the icy-cold North Sea, fully-clothed, full of drink and full of bravado. I spent the next two days in bed, trying to shake off a cold that could have easily developed into pneumonia.

The workingmen's club scene in the North of England was also really taking off, with lots of work for singers and comedians. I could have worked every afternoon and night, if I had wished. With the burgeoning club scene came new acts, new agents, and many others who wanted to cash in when the going was good.

In the hundreds of clubs across the North – at least one on every housing estate – tens of thousands of people were seeking entertainment not just at weekends but also during the week. The club was the focal point for entertainment in the local community and for club acts and agents they were a gold mine. They were also a golden opportunity for entrepreneurs with big ideas who had a lot to offer, who could earn millions.

One such entrepreneur was Vincent Francis Luvaglio, who later changed his name to Landa. Vince had arrived in the North East from London in the early 1960s and thought he had arrived in the promised land.

It was an era that promised much, plenty of work for entertainers in the cash-rich clubs and nightclubs that attracted thousands of people every night of the week, excitement, women, fast cars, new challenges and new risks, and the opportunity that could make or break a comedian's career. Myself and a number of other local entertainers teamed up with Vince Landa, and we took the North East by storm.

* * * * * * *

"You see that fella in the end bed on the ward?" I asked an old friend from the East End, George Craig, as he sat in the room on one of his many visits to see me.

"Which one. Him reading the paper?"

"That's him," I said. "He was telling me he's been in here twice before, and both times there was a Royal visit."

"Get away," said George.

"No. I'm telling you. The first time he was standing by the end of his bed when the Royal party walked around the ward and the visiting Royal asked what was wrong with him. He said 'I've got spots on my balls'.

"Why the matron went ape shit when the visit was over and told the bloke he shouldn't speak to Royalty like that. She said he should have told the Royal he had spots on his back, or his neck, or his legs.

"He was back in the same ward with the same problem the year after when another Royal was visiting and again he was asked what was wrong with him. He said 'I've got spots on my legs'. The Royal asked him 'Has the spots on your balls healed up then'?"

"Oh, my God. You're back on form," said George, laughing. "It'll not be long before you're back on the bloody Empire."

I had been in hospital for almost two weeks, and I felt a little stronger, but it would be some time before I'd be back to normal strength. The stage seemed a long way off and touring the pubs, clubs and nightclubs was now nothing more than a far distant memory.

I'd been in hospital 15 years earlier after suffering a heart attack in the bath at Diane's parents' home in East Ham, London. I was rushed to hospital, then transferred to Sunderland General and was under a heart specialist for a year before I got the all-clear. Then there was my second heart attack a few years later when I was on a tour of the Middle East with that great songstress Judith Durham. We had followed comedian Jim Davidson on to the stage and I didn't feel at all bad, but all the symptoms were there, apparently, and were spotted by a surgeon who happened to be in the audience. The surgeon visited my dressing room afterwards and asked if I had had a heart attack recently. He said he had been watching me closely and he could see a vein in my neck pumping wildly all the way through my act. He examined me there and then and I collapsed right in front of him.

I was rushed to a £650-a-day hospital where I stayed for five days and then I managed to get a flight to Heathrow which had medics on board and Judith Durham, God bless her, looked after me throughout the flight. She was a great singer and, I'm pleased to say, a great friend in my moment of need. She had to cancel half the tour because of my heart attack. At Heathrow Judith was met by her husband and I was put in a wheelchair, hoping to get a flight to Newcastle, but, in the end, I was put on a train at King's Cross instead. On the train I met players at Sunderland Football Club on their way back to the North East following an away match in the capital, and the lads took over where Judith had left off, helping me and asking about my welfare.

Either of those heart attacks could have killed me but, thankfully, I got over them. When you're hit with something like that, and get over it, it makes you believe you have been given another chance, another bite at the cherry, and it also makes you reflect on what you have done with your life. A similar contemplative mood came upon me when I was working on a cruise ship in the Mediterranean when I struck up a friendship with an old man called John Bates who did nothing else but cruise the world. He was a fantastically interesting character, with great stories to tell. I got up for breakfast one morning to find that John wasn't sitting at his usual table. He had died in his sleep during the night. Here one moment and gone the next.

I don't know what caused my heart attacks but I do know that life as a comedian can be extremely stressful, and was especially so in the tough working men's clubs in the North of England. It takes some bottle to get up on stage and try to make people laugh and many, many, comics have had moments in northern clubs they would rather forget. That great comedian Les Dawson once told me he was thinking of packing it all in after a hard night at Farringdon Social Club in Sunderland. He stayed with it, though, and became one of the greatest comedians in the country.

Off-stage, and in the confines of dressing rooms, comics on the circuit shared their own gag about the hard-to-please club audiences. A comic would say 'the good news is, they're building a tunnel under the stage at Town End Farm Working Men's Club', 'great', came the reply. 'But the bad news is,' the comic added, "it comes up at the club in Downhill'!

Chapter Eight

THE STARLINER

Bombing south down the old A1, the big, flash, sky-blue American Starliner motor I had bought from my earnings, was heavy on the fuel, but light on the eyes, and attracted stares wherever I went.

This time, however, the watchful eyes were of the old bill, and me and my travelling pal, Dennis Davies, wearing a pin-striped suit and cocked trilby hat and looking every inch the Chicago gangster, were ordered to pull over.

"Good morning, squadron leader," said the officer as I wound down the driver window. "Are you having difficulty taking off?"

It was one of the best lines I had ever heard from a police officer.

"Is this your car?" He asked.

"Yes."

"Really. So what do you do for a living?"

Before I could open my mouth, Dennis said: "We rob banks!"

"Shut your fucking mouth," I said to Dennis. "Ignore him, officer," I said. "He thinks he's a comedian."

I told the police officer who I was, where we were headed and he looked the car over, seemed happy enough with my explanations of why I was driving so fast, and allowed us to get on our way.

Dennis Davies I had known for years, having grown up with him in the East End. Like me, he came from a big family and had known the poverty that crippled people's lives just after the Second World War. We were so poor eight of us slept in one double bed, four at the top and four at the bottom. That was bad enough, but some of the kids were bed-wetters. Thankfully I always ended up sleeping in the shallow end and every morning we woke up we weren't greeted by the sun, we were greeted by a rainbow.

They say imitation is the sincerest form of flattery and in my mate Dennis Davies imitation was taken to the extremes. When I bought my white suit, he bought a white suit, if I bought suede shoes, he bought suede shoes, if I'd worn a pink fedora, he'd do the same. The guy even styled his hair like mine, and dyed it flaming red. Dennis was always on my tail, he followed me around like a pile of glue. He tried to act like me, sing like me, even dance like me. But in the end he just had to acknowledge there was only one Bobby Knoxall.

Dennis dressed like a gangster because that's what he was. A villain who carried a gun, and who wasn't afraid to use it. He blasted a shotgun at the doors of a nightclub in Darlington one night, just because they wouldn't let him in.

Dennis was an enforcer for the flamboyant, swarthy, smooth-talking entrepreneur Vincent Francis Luvaglio who had arrived in the North East in the early 1960s from London on a mission to make millions. When Vince had a meeting with the infamous Kray Twins in a café in Sunderland town centre, there was two people with him, Dennis Davies and a man who was to become a great friend of mine, Peter Hubbard. Peter was known as "the mediator" in London's gangland because he would be called in to settle disputes between warring factions. He provided a kind of arbitration service.

Vince Landa, like me, drove a big, flash, American car and, the story goes, he ended up in Sunderland by accident. He was following a coach travelling north on the A1 and thought its destination board said "Sutherland", the town in Scotland. An attractive young woman looking out of the coach rear window understandably attracted his attention and at a service station on the A1 he wooed her, screwed her, and ended up living with her in a flat in Sunderland. She took him into the Gilley Law Working Men's Club in the town, and his first question was, "where's the bandits?". Her reply was brief: "What's bandits?" She asked.

The relaxation in the gaming laws had already took hold in London and criminal gangs had seized control of the pubs and clubs to get their gaming machines, the one-armed bandits, installed. It really was a lucrative business and could legitimately earn gaming bosses tens of thousands of pounds. Illegitimately, the bandits could earn owners millions. When Vince Landa entered the Gilley Law Working Men's Club he thought he was on his way to making millions.

In the working men's clubs business was booming and trade in the town's nightclubs, The Locarno, Wetherells, The Top Rank Suite (known as The Rink), were packing them in at weekends. One nightclub, however, The Porama Club in the town's High Street West, was suffering midweek, with sometimes as few as 12 punters. Seaburn Hall was also having financial troubles, despite attracting big-name groups. Its problem was it had no bars where people could drink.

The town was still attracting big-name stars. Adam Faith, Wayne Fontana, Billy Fury all played Wetherells

The Ro Ko-Ko, for me, on the Roker seafront, was still the place to be and the place to be seen. Many entertainers packing them in at the clubs and nightclubs earlier would end up there for a late-night drink.

People wanted to be entertained, to dance, sing, and enjoy a pint, and for most the working men's clubs provided the lot. Clubs in Pallion, Red House, Town End Farm, Pennywell, Peterlee, Thorney Close, Grindon, New Herrington, Washington, Houghton, South Hetton, the River Wear Club and the Ivy Leaf in Hendon, and hundreds of others across the North East gave tens of thousands of people a great night out, to escape the drudgery of the working week in the shipyards, the pits, or wherever else they worked. It was a great time, and a money-making time, for anyone who could sing, dance or tell a few gags.

Despite the fact that the sixties were swinging and there was a new, vibrant, mood, my home town still had some old-fashioned values. Young single women weren't allowed in some of the town centre pubs unless they were accompanied by a male escort.

The Bailey Organisation, as well as owning Wetherells, had La Dolce Vita and The Cavendish in Newcastle, the Latino in South Shields, Tito's in Stockton, the Marimba and The Contessa in Middlesbrough, the La Bamba in Darlington, the La Ronde in Billingham and Dino's in Whitley Bay.

And there were other, thriving, nightclubs. Tom Jones played at The Piccadilly in Newcastle (which later became Changes owned by Vince Landa) with his minder in tow, Paddy Hallett – Irish Paddy – who later became a driver for me. Newcastle's Bird Cage nightclub was known for its card sharps.

What all the clubs and the nightclubs were crying out for was cabaret; good singers, speciality acts and good comedians who could hold an audience. For comedians like me, the little waster Bobby Thompson, Bobby Pattinson, that great comedian Tony Minchella, Raymond Hill, Rickie Price, Al Collins and singers like Jackie Longstaff and John Gaffney (stage name Johnny Dawn), we had never had it so good.

And a night out was relatively cheap. Punters could go out with one pound, pay seven-and-six to get into La Dolce Vita in Newcastle, buy a Castella cigar for half-a-crown and still have enough for four pints of beer.

Newcastle, like Sunderland, had its fair share of hard men. One who frequented La Dolce Vita was Davey Findlay. One night, outside the club, he ended up with an axe in his head and, casually, walked up to the hospital quietly asking the stunned medical staff if they could kindly take it out.

Davey was minder for Ray Graham, who owned other nightclubs in Newcastle, The Downbeat and The Gogo, and The Crescendo in Whitley Bay. When Ray opened a nightclub up in London, The Krays told him to get back to the North East and Davey was tied to a chair and had seven bells kicked out of him. In a criminal underworld where reputations are earned in practise, rather than earned by reputation, Davey became a friend in the north to The Krays. The Krays did visit Newcastle, but left in a hurry.

The cabaret in La Dolce Vita, in Newcastle's Blackfriars Street, was a big American star called Billy Eckstine. A regular customer, who had a permanent reserved table for ten, was one of Vince Landa's cash collectors, Angus Sibbet. Angus was a larger-than-life character with a wife and children, a big house in Gateshead, two mistresses (sisters from Sunderland), and what appeared to be a never ending flow of cash. When he and his guests got to their table they would follow the paymaster. If he ordered a Bacardi and Coke, everyone else would have a Bacardi and Coke. If he ordered a fillet steak, everyone else would have a fillet steak. He was like the king at his table.

When I played the clubs in Newcastle, I would end up, as late as three in the morning, in Bowers café, opposite the city's central railway station. Many other entertainers would end up there, such as Bobby Pattinson, who would arrive in a white Mercedes Benz. And I would also re-acquaint myself with some of the lads I had met when I worked on the barrows, like the Tamseys, the Kellys, and the Sayers brothers and George "Blower" Shotton, Panda Anderson, and other well-known Newcastle hard-men.

Vince Landa opened his offices for Social Club Services Limited in Sunderland town centre and what he offered the clubs and nightclubs was something unique; a full entertainment package which included cabaret, singers and comedians like myself, in some cases he offered to fit-out the clubs, and, of course, installing the one-armed bandits, which ended up paying for the cabaret. It was a huge operation which ended up covering all the working men's clubs from the Scottish border down to the border with North Yorkshire.

Myself, Tony Minchella, Rickie Price, Al Collins, Jackie Longstaff, Johnny Dawn, Raymond Hill, were just a few of the entertainers on Vince's books. On the nightclub scene he had his friend Dennis Stafford, a convicted criminal who had made a daring escape from Dartmoor Prison and saw his co-escapee drown, who was living with a beautiful, black, nightclub singer, Salena Jones, and his brother Michael Luvaglio, a quiet, unassuming, man, who had little to say, was also a well-known face on the nightclub scene. As well as his office in Sunderland, Vince had a small office in Albert Road, Middlesbrough, which was run by Davey Snowball, a salesman he employed who lived in Sacriston, County Durham.

Vince Landa's manager cum accountant, Bill Thompson, was one of his main men, as was George Wilson, and both men I was later pleased to count as my friends. Ray Thubron, a miner, also teamed up with Vince and Ray soon upgraded his car from a Morris Minor type to something a little more flash. Jimmy and Geordie Laws, cousins of my great friend Dickie Laws, were also on Vince's pay-roll.

Ray Thubron's brother Bobby ran an artiste's agency, known as the

North Star Agency, and his was one of many agencies springing up in the boom-time of the mid 1960s when people with the right connections knew there was money to be made, and how to make it. The agencies wanted stars on their books, to manage them, book them into clubs and to make themselves some money through their ten or 15 per cent cut. Agents popped up in Sunderland like Doris and Tommy Bogey and Norman Fassa and Ronnie Prenelle, who ran an agency in Paley Street.

Landa offered clubs a full package of entertainment, fitting out the clubs if that was needed, cabaret acts, singers, dancers, comedians like myself and, of course, the main money-maker, the one-armed bandits. He brought a chap called Larry Hill up from Sheffield to run the entertainment side of the business and Larry would allocate jobs to us.

The bandits were, of course, fixed to earn as much money as possible for those involved in the business. That was how Vince became a millionaire several times over and his business colleague Angus Sibbet could afford to have his own table reserved every night of the week in any one of a number of nightclubs, such as La Dolce Vita, The Piccadily or The Bird Cage in Newcastle.

Me, I just told gags at the clubs I was assigned to go to. But other entertainers - singer John Gaffney and comedian Al Collins were among them - did a little work for Vince collecting tanners (sixpences) from the fixed machines in some of the hundreds of workingmen's clubs in which Vince's salesmen had managed to get them installed.

During the mid to late 1960s I met and worked with some of the greatest entertainers I had the pleasure to meet, all professionals, and many who became good friends. I worked with a group of dwarfs, known as the Mini-Tones, who played Wetherells in Sunderland, some of whom went on to get parts in Star Wars, and with Lynn Perrie, who had one of the best singing voices I had ever heard. Lynn went on to greater things as Ivy Tildsley in that great TV soap institution Coronation Street.

Vince Landa's one-armed bandit empire went belly-up when Angus Sibbet was found dead with three bullets in his body, lying on the back seat of a Mark 10 Jaguar parked underneath Pesspool Bridge in South Hetton, a mining village in County Durham, in early January, 1967.

I was playing the East End Social Club in Sunderland the Sunday lunchtime after the murder, and it was the talk of the place. The shooting dead of a playboy found slumped in a flash car in a little-known mining village was front page news and South Hetton Workmen's Club, where Peter McCarron played the organ at the weekends, was buzzing with the gossip.

Vince's business associates, his brother Michael Luvaglio and Dennis Stafford, boyfriend of the beautiful, black, nightclub singer Salena Jones, were arrested, charged, and, ultimately, convicted of the murder of Angus Sibbet, but protested their innocence from day one and still protest their innocence today. The case threw up many unanswered questions, resulted in appeal after appeal, and sparked the cult movie classic Get Carter, loosely based on what was the North East's most notorious and controversial murder cases.

Several of Vince Landa's business associates were arrested and quizzed. One of them was Davey Snowball, who had, the night before, been involved in a scrap at The Marimba Club in Middlesbrough, and opened his front door in Sacriston still wearing his white dress shirt, which had bloodstains on it. Davey had some explaining to do.

I had many dealings with Vince Landa and met his brother Michael and Dennis Stafford, and Angus Sibbet, many times, during the time I worked for Vince. I never had any problems with Vince Landa, who always paid the entertainers in full and on time. The murder was a curious affair, not least because a motive for the killing was never clearly established. If two men were wrongly convicted, we might never know.

And I wasn't to know, at that time, that my path and those of two people I met and liked associated with the case, would cross again, linked to nightclubs, entertainment and yet more foreign travel.

* * * * * * *

The craving for a fag really was temptation beyond endurance. Ten fags sat in the top drawer of my utility cupboard at the side of my hospital bed and, bloody hell, there was even a disposable lighter in the same drawer, put there by my brother Charlie. I'd gone without a cigarette for several days and the craving for a quick dose of nicotine was kicking in so hard I felt like lighting up there and then in the room, and bugger the consequences. But there were rules, which I could understand, and there was my post-operative health and well-being, which I could understand, and there was the fire risk, which I could also understand. But, for God's sake, there was also 10 Embassy Regal king size in the drawer inches away from my bed. The temptation, the test of will-power, could only be understood by the hardened smoker used to going through at least 40 cigarettes a day, which I had done, apart from the last few days, for more than 50 years.

For the first time the wheelchair at the other side of my hospital bed, looked inviting and the whole scenario appeared to be a challenge; a challenge for me to get up off my arse, out of the bed, into the wheel-chair, and away to that social leper's paradise, in the open-air, outside the hospital, in the cool night air, where I could inhale nicotine to my heart's content without upsetting my neighbours and without the risk of their lungs being contaminated, passively, by my abhorrent, socially-repellent, filthy, mucky, habit of enjoying a cigarette.

Challenge on, I thought.

It was approaching midnight, most people on the ward were asleep, and as I clumsily lifted my body from the skin-clinging mattress and clutched my urine bottle, I turned myself around, sat on the edge of the bed, and grabbed the fags and lighter from the cupboard. In a manoeu-vre that took all the strength I had, I grabbed the handrails of the wheel-chair and slowly lifted myself from the bed, plonking my arse into the cool plastic wheelchair seat, clinging on to it as if losing my grip meant the difference between life and death.

Then I was seated, I was mobile … and I was away.

I pushed the wheels, cruised along the corridor, and for the first time for approaching a week, I felt my independence; that free-wheeling spir-it of individuality that tells you you are a human being, you are unique.

"Are you going down?" Asked a middle-aged woman as I approached the lift.

"Yes," I said. "Ground floor."

When we reached the ground floor the woman pushed me in my wheelchair to the hospital exit door, which slid open automatically, and for the first time in many days I inhaled the cool night air, looked up at the stars, and thanked God, and the surgeons at Sunderland General Hospital, that I was still alive.

Then I grabbed my ten fags and my lighter and, one by one, I smoked all ten cigarettes. It was a selfish act, where I had given in to an overwhelming craving that had consumed my thoughts. I was spaced out. And, for the first time, I realised the potency of nicotine as a drug, and I could, again for the first time, sympathise with alcoholics and drug addicts whose cravings go far beyond those of a smoker.

Despite the warnings from the doctors, I had succumbed to my personal failings by smoking fags. But I didn't half enjoy them. The doctors would shake their heads, frown with disapproval, and castigate me verbally. But the ciggies, I believed, were just another stage in my rehabilitation.

Was I on the mend? And would I once again grace the stage of some working men's club or a theatre, to do what I was best at, stand up comedy?

Time, I thought, would tell.

Chapter Nine

THE COCK O' THE NORTH

The stripper, Mizzi, like many other strippers, had a great stage presence. It probably had something to do with the fact that she took all her clothes off, seductively, sensuously and rhythmically. Throughout her act Mizzi had one main prop, a cat. She called the cat her pussy, and left little to the imagination.

My travelling companion, a talented singer who shall remain nameless, had fallen for Mizzi's pussy in a big way. He didn't like the cat. Their affair was, from his accounts only, torrid, rampant and involved sexual athletics on an Olympic scale that produced much sweat and carpet burns.

He screwed her by night, and he screwed her by day, and over breakfast in our lodgings his face looked sunny-side up. His eggs were poached, his bacon was rindless, his toast was well done and his coffee always strong.

We'd been performing at a club in Manchester, stayed the night in our lodgings, and were due back up in the North East that night. We had taken the clubs of Yorkshire, Lancashire and Manchester, by storm, and knew we would be welcomed back.

During our stay in Manchester Dusty Springfield held a big party in her large, private, house, and issued an edict to all those in show-business working in the area at the time: "Don't tell them Geordie bastards."

Dusty, like most other people unaware of the geography of the North East, labelled everyone from the region a Geordie, whether they were from Newcastle, Sunderland, Middlesbrough or Alnwick.

My friend and I were a bit put out at not getting an invite to Dusty's big bash, but we turned up anyway and, hoping to make something of an entrance, we knocked on the door of the big, palatial, mansion with our balls hanging out. My mate's left hand covered my privates, and my right hand covered his, and when the door was opened by some big, butch, lesbian-type, I lifted my right hand to say "this is", announcing his name, and he lifted his left hand and said: "This is… Bobby Knoxall".

We gate-crashed the party, but didn't stay long. It really wasn't our cup of tea. The house was full of homosexuals and lesbians and, though I have never had anything against gays, my mate and I felt a little out of place, being heterosexual and looking for a female hump for the night.

At our lodgings my mate joined me for breakfast and I was reading my newspaper. All the newspapers that day were dominated by one main story, the capture of Harry Roberts, who had been on the run for more than three months after the gunning down of three police officers in cold blood in a quiet street in London near Shepherd's Bush.

"I see they've caught Harry Roberts," I said to my mate.

"Really?" He said. "Where's he been hiding out? The Ivy Leaf Social Club?"

"No," I said. "According to this here newspaper he's been kipping in a barn in the countryside."

"There's something else you'll find interesting," I said.

"What's that then?" Asked my mate.

"His wife's a stripper."

"And why would that interest me?"

"Because this here stripper is called Mizzi and she performs on stage with a cat."

My mate's face turned a ghostly shade of white. He almost choked on his cornflakes.

"You what. You fucking what! You're winding me up!" He exclaimed.

"It's all here in black and white," I said, and threw the newspaper on to the table in front of him.

He read the story, quietly ... then jumped up from the table so quickly he knocked his chair over, knocked my fresh cup of tea over, and ran out of the dining room like a dog that had just had a red-hot poker thrust up it's arse.

"Fuck this!" He shouted. "Fuck this!"

A few minutes later he was back in the dining room, his case packed, sweating like the proverbial pig and panting so hard I thought he was risking a heart attack.

"Ha'way, we're going," he said.

"Fuck that," I said. "I haven't finished my tea."

"Fuck your tea," he said. "We're leaving. Now!"

And that was it. Goodbye Manchester, hello Sunderland. We hit the old A1 burning rubber and ended back at home in record time.

My mate was a married man with children, and, by this time, so was I, but the sense of freedom we enjoyed was something other married men could only dream about. The clubs and the cabaret rooms were dripping with gorgeous-looking, slim-figured and, best of all, available, women who were not shy at coming forward. My mate was like a dog with two knobs and my own was getting plenty of exercise. If regular exercise builds muscle, I had a very strong muscle.

It was about this time that I met one of the most talented singers on the club circuit that I had ever seen. For a woman petite in stature she had a powerful and melodic voice and the knack of connecting with her audience. We teamed up on stage a few times, and we teamed up off-stage quite regularly. Our affair lasted quite some time. I later headed back up north and started my foreign travels and this little lady went on to become a top star in one of Britain's best loved soaps.

Life, for my mate and I, was one big adventure and when we hit the road to head south that sense of freedom really struck home when we reached a pub called The Cock o' The North, in Durham, heading for the old A1 after the three-mile limit.

"Yippee!" My mate would shout. "Yippee", and we would be off, heading for the clubs in Yorkshire, Lancashire, Wales, or London. Coincidentally, and somewhat flatteringly, the name of the pub became synonymous with Bobby Knoxall among the dancers, strippers, and female hangers-on who frequented the clubs and were up for sex. It wasn't so much casual sex, there was nothing casual about it, it was just pure, unadulterated, no-holds-barred, highly-charged shagging. Day and night, night and day. A girl in every port.

One stripper I had the pleasure of had such an insatiable sexual appetite that she almost shagged me out, but, as ever, I stayed the distance. Like I did on stage, I always gave my best in any performance.

Later the next day my mate and I sat down with a drink to watch a blue movie and the star of the hardcore show was none other than … the stripper I had shagged the previous day.

Some of the strippers I worked with, such as two who were employed by the Gateshead-based Anne Robinson Agency, were pure artistes who knew how to strip and who knew how to tease an audience, but others were just women who took their clothes off to music for money. One used to do the dance of the seven virgins, all down to memory, of course, and there was an Indian stripper, a real dusky maiden, who danced over a bowl of curry. We used to call it the dance of the curry with the minge on top.

Stripping, of course, can be a risky business, the girls seemed to have little protection from perverts and low-lifes. I worked with a stripper called Julie Perigo several times, she was a nice lass, also employed by the Anne Robinson Agency. Julie was found murdered in her flat in Downhill, Sunderland, and her killer has never been caught.

Later I teamed up again with my great mate Jackie Longstaff and we built up a strong and, I think, deserved reputation as one of the best acts in club-land. We only had one pair of patent leather shoes between us which had holes in the soles and cardboard for insoles. Jackie used to say when our soles left our uppers we'd be on our feet again. The fashionable item at the time was mohair suits, but Jackie was still in a barathea blazer and I was still into evening suits. We had to keep up with the times, so we both bought ourselves a suit length of mohair at a market in Barnsley and got a tailor in Sheffield to run them up, so we could take to the stage looking smart and up-to-date. Mohair was very shiny material and it looked the business, the only problem was the material split very easily and patches had to be ironed rather than sewn on to cover the holes. After our stage act Jackie and I would go into the audience and talk to the people who had watched the show, but we would always end up with a hole in our suits. It got so bad that we both ended up with big holes in the seats of our pants and, when we took a bow, we had to walk off the stage backwards!

Business in club-land had peaked and Jackie and I were in big demand. And so were other stars, comics and singers, Tony Minchella, Johnny Duffy, Alan Fox, Bobby Pattinson, Ricky Price, to name but a few, and the grand master of North East comedy Bobby Thompson who could play any club he liked and invariably did. If he was to receive £13 and the other club in which he was booked that night was only paying him £12, he would always go to the club paying the extra quid.

Johnny Hammond was also a well-liked club comedian. He once played the Downhill Club in Sunderland when the club was surrounded by cops and a man sitting on his own in the audience was carrying a gun he had just used to blow a relation's head off. When the cops eventually stormed the place, after a stand-off of about half-an-hour, and led the gunman away, Johnny shouted: "Can't you take these bastards as well!"

Bobby Thompson was a great North East comedian and he was happy to stay in the North East where he had earned himself a big following. His act was very regional and would not appeal to a national or international audience.

Other comedians were also happy to stay in the North East. But me? I'd been bitten by the travelling bug and, even though my accent was very much Mackem, I knew I could make it wherever I went, with the right attitude and the right delivery.

The clubs were great and my fellow comedians and other artistes were talented people, easy to get along with, and I could have stayed in the North East forever, earning decent money. But I was becoming disillusioned with taking orders from agents to drive to this club and that, living out of suitcases in hotels and bed and breakfast guest houses, seeing little of my family. It was this being away from home for lengthy periods that really destroyed my first marriage, a marriage which produced four children.

Basically, I wanted to do what I wanted to do, not what other people thought best for me. I didn't want to just stand on stage in North East working men's clubs and tell gags. I wanted to expand my horizons and live a little by travelling to other parts of the world.

But, wherever my career was to take me, I knew that I would always end up back in my hometown of Sunderland, the town where I was born and where I put down roots.

For me Sunderland has never just been a large seaside town in the North East of England – it has always been the centre of my universe.

* * * * * * *

The strain on my body was enormous as I slowly lifted myself from the bed, put my skinny, long, feet on the floor and reached for the walking frame in front of me. It was one small step for Bobby Knoxall but one giant leap in my rehabilitation.

"You're standing, Bob! You're standing!" Exclaimed a jubilant Diane walking into the room clutching a bag of grapes and a bottle of Lucozade.

"Take it easy. Take it easy," she said.

I was taking it easy. With all my strength, much of which had been drained from my body through the aneurysm and the subsequent operation, I threw the walking frame just a few inches in front of me, then dragged my almost lifeless legs forward. Diane put the grapes and drink on the bed and stood behind me, with her arm on my right shoulder.

"Where are you going?" She asked.

"I need some fresh air and I could do with some company", I said. "I've been stuck in here for days. I just need a change of scenery."

"Use the wheelchair," said Diane.

"Fuck the wheelchair," I said. "I want to walk. I'm not bothered if it kills me. I'm going to walk."

With a jolt I again threw the four-legged aluminium frame in front of me, and moved forward, just a few inches. The pain was excruciating but my determination unshakeable. After a few minutes I was away from my own room, entering the main ward and, for the first time for months, there, right in front of me, was an audience.

"Go on Bobby!" Said a man in the first bed, sitting up.

"Bye, you look bloody ill," I said. "My dad's in a better shape than you are, and we buried him two weeks ago."

The ward erupted in laughter.

I staggered slowly along the ward, as the other patients shouted encouragement, and came to rest at the foot of a man's bed who was sitting up in a chair, right in front of my path.

"Are you in show-business?" I asked.

"No", said the bloke.

"Then get your fucking chair off my stage."

"Here, Bobby," said another man. "How's the family?"

"They're great. They're doing great." I said.

"This is my lovely wife Diane, and we've got four big, strapping sons at home.

"I spotted the youngest up to his eyes in muck the other day playing with a jar of liquid in the gutter. I said what's that you're playing with. He said sulphuric acid. I said sulphuric acid, you can't play with that. He said hang on, I don't tell you what to do with your holy water.

"I said, son, I sprinkled a lady's tummy with that holy water the other day, and she passed a baby.

" 'That's nowt', the boy said, 'I sprinkled this on the dog's bollocks, and he passed a Ferrari'."

The ward was in hysterics now.

"Have you got any bairns?" I asked a bloke sitting in bed reading a newspaper.

"Aye. I've got two," he said proudly.

"Two? Bloody hell," I said. "I did better than that when I was single."

"Here, youngen," I said to a lad aged about 20 sitting on the other side of the ward.

"Have you seen that fella in The Bridges who pretends he's fishing. He just stands there every day, casting off with his imaginary fishing line. Have you seen him?"

"No," the young lad said.

"Well. I was standing in The Bridges with my mate and we were looking at him and I thought, poor bloke, he must be mentally ill. He must be from Cherry Knowle Hospital. I felt really sorry for him, everyone staring at him and that, so I went up to him and gave him a tenner. 'Have you caught owt?' I asked. 'Aye', said the fella, 'you're the tenth today'."

The laughing patients broke into a round of applause, and I turned to make my way back to my room.

"Go on Bobby," said one. "Go on my son."

The short journey back with the aid of the walking frame appeared easier on my legs and, after weeks of pain, idleness, painkillers, physiotherapy, tests, more tests, and feeling as much use as a chocolate fireguard, my spirits had lifted.

As Diane helped me back into bed, she said: "You feel any better for that?"

"I do," I said. "And it proves one thing to me. Laughter really is the best medicine."

Chapter Ten
THE SUMMER OF '69

I had died a death. Never before had I failed to connect with an audience, never before had the silence from the crowd been so deafening or the applause at the end so muted. The critic on the local newspaper had had a field day, launching into a scathing tirade and I felt my career as a globe-trotting international comedy cabaret star was over even before it had begun.

I sat at a table in the bar of La Belle Etoile, a hotel and cabaret room in Jersey, and my only companions were my old mate Ron Bacardi and an unashamedly effeminate, openly homosexual, choreographer, called Ken Wayne, who was giving me a sympathetic hearing. He didn't have to listen to my self-pitying moans, but he did, and I was grateful.

"I don't have to put up with this shit, from these shit people," I said. "In the North East I'm a comedy legend. I've had enough of this crap. I don't fucking need it."

"They're not shit people," said Ken. "They've come to see you in one of the best hotels in one of the best resorts in the country, and you're just not good enough."

His straight-talking hurt.

"You were crap. You were fucking crap," said Ken.

"I know I was fucking crap," I said. "But where did I go wrong? I've never bombed like that before. What happened?"

"Everything you did was wrong." Said Ken. "You speak too fast. You're accent is far too broad. You walk on stage wrong. You stand wrong. Your clothes are wrong. Your hair's a mess and, despite your best efforts old boy, you didn't make a link with the audience. They couldn't understand you.

"You have no discipline. You're just a very raw comedian from Geordieland, and the clubs are all you're used to. This is a production, where discipline is everything. It's not some spit-and-sawdust club in the arse-end of Sunderland."

Here I was sitting at a hotel bar table after my first night on the cabaret scene on a summer season in Jersey that had promised so much, drowning my sorrows with a bottle of Bacardi and taking a load of shit from a raving queer. If the poor excuse for a man wasn't so fragile I could have snapped him in half.

It had all started a few months earlier at the Blue Star Club in Newcastle where the producer of the show, called Grin and Tonic, in Jersey, Frank Thomasson, and the director Dick Ray, were up in the North East looking for talent.

I'd gone along to the auditions, like I did at all auditions, hoping for the best but not expecting too much. We were told the show needed one comedian to top the bill and there were several auditioning, including an old acquaintance Alan Fox, from South Shields, who started off singing but later turned full-time comic and impressionist.

Alan, who was born in Tyne Dock and attended St Bede's Roman Catholic School in the town, had fought his way up the ladder much in the same way as I had. He entered talent shows and got something of a break when Frankie Vaughan visited the Tyne Dock Boys' Club in Shields and he was asked by the big star to do an impression of him. Alan did Give Me The Moonlight and Frankie Vaughan fell about laughing he was so impressed. Alan went to the Royal Festival Hall in London with all the other regional talent show winners for the national final and ended up on stage with Frankie Vaughan, Vera Lynne and Billy Cotton. At the end of the show, in which he was runner-up, Alan went on stage for the final bow – which he was not meant to do – and he appeared in the photo that ended up in the New Musical Express.

His talent as an impressionist grew, along with his repertoire of gags, and Alan, like myself, toured all the clubs in the North East and the big clubs elsewhere. The Scala Club in Doncaster was considered the 'Palladium of the North', where both Alan and I starred, and other top clubs in Yorkshire included The Ace Club in Wakefield, the Ace of Clubs in Leeds and the Greasebrough in Rotherham. Alan played alongside some big stars; David Whitfield, Ronnie Hilton, Roy Orbison, Sasha Distelle, Alma Cogan, to name but a few. Like me Alan was also managed at one time by Bob Deplidge, who also managed stars such as The

Krankies, Dustin Gee, Tony Stewart and Colin Price.

At the Newcastle auditions we both did very well and it appeared to be a two-horse race to the finish, but Frank Thomasson and Dick Ray only wanted one comedian for the show. Frank wanted me to top the bill and Dick wanted Alan Fox. Unusually they decided to give a contract to both of us for the summer season in Jersey, with myself topping the bill. I saw it as a great opportunity and one that would give a welcome boost to my career in show-business. All I needed to do was do well.

As I chatted to Ken Wayne, slightly inebriated having almost gone through a bottle of Bacardi, I realised that in allowing my East End macho prejudices to surface I had done the man a great disservice. Here was a man who had worked with some of the biggest stars in the world, who had a track record in London's West End which many other choreographers would die for, and who would have ranked alongside Fred Astaire and Gene Kelly as one of the world's greatest dancers, had he been in the right place at the right time. The man was an artist, with such an extended imagination he could make a silk purse out of a sow's ear. He was also a man who could, as was proven, take a raggy-arsed, uncouth, undisciplined, brawling, lanky, rough-edged, streetfighting, in-your-face, hard-case North East club comedian and turn him into an international comedy cabaret star almost overnight.

As I sat at the bar table and listened intently, I was given an education. I learned more that one night from this man I initially dismissed as nothing more than a "puff", than I had ever learned in my life, at school, on the barrows, in the Army, on the streets, in the clubs or from any of my many agents. Ken told me a little about his history and I was enthralled. I also felt profoundly guilty that I had allowed my pre-conceptions to misjudge the man so very badly.

He had become immersed in the theatre and dancing from a very early age and had sold buckets of manure he collected in "posh" areas near his East End London home to pay for his own tap dancing lessons. His love of dancing started the day he went to see Top Hat, starring Fred Astaire and Ginger Rogers, at his local cinema. Afterwards he danced all the way home.

His parents never encouraged him to follow a career in the theatre and, indeed, his father forced him to work in the factory where he worked after he left school, but Ken just stood on the factory floor for three weeks with his arms folded until the company was forced to sack him.

Like me he had served time in the services, in his case the Royal Air Force, and like me he was discharged with ignominy. But, whereas I was discharged for fighting, and a conviction for affray, Ken was discharged after he told senior officers he was a homosexual. His discharge from the RAF only followed a series of humiliating and degrading interviews and examinations which, said Ken, made him feel like a criminal. In those days, of course, homosexuality was illegal.

His father thought dancing was "a puff's game" and Ken had a difficult childhood. When he told me something of his history I knew in later years when a movie was shot in the North East, that he was the original and real Billy Elliott, the character from the movie of the same name who battled prejudice and bigotry to do what he does best, dance.

Ken lived in the same street as Alfred Hitchcock, who had by then made his name in Hollywood, and Hitchcock had attended the same school he had, though more than two decades earlier.

Despite his father's unwavering opposition to his son's wishes to go into the theatre, and perhaps because of it, Ken Wayne became a pretty big star, moving up through amateur theatres to being the second lead male dancer in The Palace Theatre in London's Shaftesbury Avenue in the hit musical The Song of Norway.

He worked with Mike and Bernie Winters, Frank Ifield – who shared his dressing room - Dick Emery, Frankie Howerd, Gracie Fields, Danny Kaye, Max Bygraves, Max Miller, and choreographed shows for Ken Williams, Lena Horne, and that world-famous artiste Sabrina, in Australia and Las Vegas.

"Did I ever tell you I met Betty Davies," said Ken, as our conversation drifted into the early hours of the morning.

"No," I said.

"She was being interviewed by the BBC in an office in Fleet Street and, as I collect autographs, I went to see her at about 8.30pm that night. The limousine pulled up. She got out, and told me I would have to wait to get anything signed. I did wait and she emerged from the radio interview at about 11.30pm, amid a lot of commotion."

"What was the commotion?" I asked.

"She wasn't happy with the interview and was telling everyone to 'fuck off'."

"Did you get your autograph?" I asked.

"Yes," said Ken. "She was very pleasant with me and said, 'haven't you been waiting such a long time', before she signed my book, a photograph, and then was driven off in the limo, waving to me like Royalty."

It was a funny story. Ken told me Betty Davies was publicising the movie Death on the Nile at the time.

Ken told me that when he first saw me walk through the doors of La Belle Etoile with my entourage, which included my mate Dennis Davies, he thought 'what on earth is that' and was not immediately enamoured with the fact that I would be topping the bill on his show.

Over the first few days of my summer season in Jersey Ken Wayne picked me up, shook me down, and transformed my image almost overnight. Gone was the old suit and in its place were tight-fitting, brightly-coloured, superbly-tailored and eye-catching three-piece suits in yellow, light blue and pink, with glitter-trimmed waistcoats. I threw out my flat shoes and replaced them with three-inch high Cuban-heeled boots that took my lanky 6ft 2ins frame to an even lankier 6ft 5ins. Out went the old non-descript hairstyle and my long, red, curly hair was brushed up and out into a mad, outrageous, Zulu-style cut that was more shocking than it was de rigueur. Ken taught me how to walk on stage, how to stand on stage, how to act on stage and how to speak, slowly and deliberately with a more refined accent, and just a hint of Mackem, which would mean I could be heard and understood. Then there was the mannerisms, those little movements of the hands and the face that take a funny gag from being just a funny gag to an hilarious moment. Ken also taught me how to dance, properly, not like doing the rock 'n roll that I had known and was good at strutting my stuff in The

Rink in Sunderland, or jumping from the mantlepiece at the town's Norfolk Hotel and doing the splits, but dance that was choreographed, timed to perfection.

I had never enjoyed taking orders in my life. I didn't like taking instructions. That would be like admitting that what I was doing was wrong, and I knew I was a good comic, if not the best. But I was happy taking my orders from Ken Wayne and within 48 hours that one man had created the new Bobby Knoxall, a comedian with the same talent, but with a new, improved, image and a new confidence and self-belief. He had taken a raw club comedian and turned him into a professional cabaret star.

The newspaper critic was invited along to La Belle Etoile to see my performance again. He was absolutely amazed by the transformation and said so when he wrote up his critique.

The new Bobby Knoxall had arrived, and the audiences loved him.

Grin and Tonic, staged and choreographed by Ken Wayne, produced by Frank Thomasson and directed by Dick Ray, proved a massive hit in Jersey in 1969. The fact that it was a major success was due to the production team, particularly Ken Wayne, and to the cast, which, as well as yours truly, featured that great singer Stuart Gillies, songstress Robin Brett, comedian Alan Fox and the fantastic Ken Wayne Dancers who performed superbly under the maestro's disciplined instructions and tutelage.

For me, 1969 was a great year, because, with the help of Ken Wayne, I discovered myself on the beautiful Channel Island of Jersey and won two top awards, as the island's Best Newcomer and as show-business Personality of the Year, awarded by the Jersey Press, and our show was voted the best on the island.

Despite my new, refreshing and colourful image I still retained at least two of my character traits that I had always been renowned for; fighting and shagging. One night I kicked seven bells out of my mate Dennis Davies, who was setting his lip up, and as for shagging ... well, let's just say Jersey was full of attractive women, visiting the island or working in the shows, who enjoyed good sex lives.

How long my wild days would last, I didn't know, but I was about to be hit by the type of transverse force that can turn a person's world upside down in an instant.

* * * * * * *

The doctor was on his morning rounds, going from bed to bed, followed by a group of about six young trainee doctors and the ward sister. He seemed in a good mood, making a few wisecracks, and his underlings would laugh in that sycophantic way underlings do when their boss cracks a joke, whether it was funny or not.

"Good morning Mr Knoxall," he said. "And how are you this glorious morning?"

"All the better for seeing you, doctor," I said. The underlings laughed.

"And are you eating?" He asked.

"Oh yes doctor," I said. "Last night I had steak Diane, with vegetables, in a nice white wine sauce with a hint of garlic, washed down with a nice, fruity Beaujolais, followed by lemon sorbet for afters."

"You're such a joker, Bobby, such a joker," the doctor said, patronisingly.

I wasn't eating. I was still drinking a lot of tea and a lot of lemonade, and all that liquid quickly filled my catheter bag. It was very strange having a pee but not depositing it in the loo until some time later. Carrying a plastic bag full of urine around wasn't the most edifying aspect of my post-operative rehabilitation, but it was part of the process, whether I liked it or not. There were people in the hospital far worse off than myself. Some would never see the outside world again.

I was feeling a little better, having made the effort to stand on my own two feet, even if it was with the aid of a walking frame, and for the past couple of days I had been sneaking along, at a snail's pace, to a rarely-used toilet for a quick, relaxing, cigarette. Even though I had been at death's door, I couldn't pack the fags in. To some people that might suggest I'm weak-willed, but to other hardened smokers who can't give up the weed, it is an indication of the power of the little coffin stick and what kind of control it can exert on those who succumb to its highly-addictive charms. I'm not proud of being a heavy smoker. Like millions of others, I'm just a nicotine addict.

Telephone calls had been coming in from far and wide from people asking how I was, people I had worked with in the past, friends, Sunderland footballers past and present, other comedians, among them my good mate Mike Reid – old Frank Butcher from Eastenders – Frank Carson, Freddie Starr.

I felt privileged to have worked with such talented people and thankful that I still had some very good friends who had stuck with me through thick and thin and watched my career progress. Among them Bill Tipling, a great character from Hendon, Colin Noble, a well-known local businessman, car dealer Graham Stephenson, publican Sammy Doran, businessman Dougie Parker and many, many more.

I had always known, but as I lay in the hospital bed realised more now than ever, that in your time of greatest need you find out who your real friends are. People matter. The outward signs of wealth or even success don't matter when it comes to the crunch; these signs are as shallow as the lake in Sunderland's Mowbray Park and the people that display them know the cost of everything, but the value of nothing. I would far sooner be a skint comedian with true friends, than a millionaire with all the trappings of success but with only arse-lickers to share it with.

I was feeling a little fitter physically and, mentally, my mind was as sharp as ever. I was on the road to recovery. All I needed to do was continue the fight back... and I was fully prepared to fight with all my might.

Top: With my friend and copycat, Dennis Davies, who was also one-time minder for Vince Landa.

Left: My good friend George Craig, from Sunderland's East End, who, despite his criminal past, built up the biggest and most successful charity for the homeless and needy in the North East, and an award-winning centre for recovering alcoholics and drug addicts.

CELEBRITIES ONE AND ALL

With Tommy Cooper (above) and (below) Vince Hill and a young hopeful.

Top: The man who had the biggest influence on my career in showbusiness, Ken Wayne, with Andrew Lloyd Webber.

Below left: I receive a comedy award from Salena Jones in Africa (the girlfriend of Dennis Stafford).

Below: A cabaret sensation, Little Mo, The Mighty Atom, lead dancer with The Roly Polys.

MY FAMILY

Diane and I with our four sons, Robert, John, Ryan and Brent.

Diane and I when I still had hair.

OLD ACQUAINTANCES

Top: One of Sunderland's earliest agents to the artiste Ronnie Prenelle (top left) with his wife Veronica, and myself (on right) with friends in The Malibu Hotel in Durban, South Africa.

Left: Sunderland millionaire entrepreneur Mattie Roseberry, who built up a pub and hotel empire from nothing.

THE FOOTBALL CONNECTION

With members of Sunderland's FA Cup winning squad in 1973 after we cut the hit single Sunderland All The Way

Below: With "Super-mac" Malcolm MacDonald and my great friend Jackie Longstaff.

Above: With the big man, Niall Quinn, former Irish international.

Left: With Charlie Hurley, Bob Cass, and "The Messiah" Bob Stokoe.

Bottom: With Peter Reid and Charlie Hurley.

THE ENTERTAINERS

With Bobby Denver (top), and
his wife Coco, Johnny Duffy
(left), Johnny Hammond
(bottom left) and at a sports-
mens' dinner (below)
with strongman-act Tony Brutus.

Chapter Eleven
LONDON CALLING

The bright lights of London had always attracted northerners, like moths to a candle on a dark night, and for comedians and other artistes looking for a decent living, the temptation of the capital, where everything happened and happened quickly, was often a temptation beyond endurance. But there were risks. Making it big in the grim-up north did not mean you could make it big in the gold-paved capital and where many had tried and succeeded, hundreds of others had tried and failed.

The first time I was drawn to London was when, as a callow youth, I ran off with my boss Richie Greenwell's £35 takings for the day on the barrows and legged it to the train station, heading for King's Cross full of optimism and the kind of teenage enthusiasm that is often blinkered to reality. I sang a few songs in pubs in Shepherd's Bush, slept rough for a few nights, then soon got the train back home. It was an experience, but nothing more.

But, these days, after a highly successful season in Jersey and having made it big in clubs not just in the north but across the country, I had a name. The name was Bobby Knoxall.

I performed for the players at Tottenham Hotspur Football Club and was later approached by Bertie Green to play the prestigious Astor Club, associated with many of London's top names in the field of show-business and also associated with some of London's top villains.

I spent a few weeks at The Astor, as Master of Ceremonies and resident comedian, and it was there that I first met Peter Hubbard, known as The Mediator, the man who would arbitrate in disputes that threatened to run to bloody violence in London's volatile criminal underworld.

My show-business mentor Ken Wayne, knew London like the back of his hand and had once put on a production at a very expensive restaurant cum cabaret establishment, Le Pigalle, in the west end, which attracted all the top stars and the cream of London's gang leaders.

Top American singer, dancer and all-round performer Sammy Davies Jnr played at Le Pigalle and I joined him and his extensive entourage for a delicious meal, plenty of drink, and fascinating conversation – and they didn't even know me.

I had been hanging around the restaurant, ticket-less and without a pot to piss in, when two long white limousines pulled up, parked, and as the chauffeur opened the near passenger door, out got Sammy Davies, his minders, his friends and his hangers on and the outside passenger door of one of the limousines opened, and in popped Bobby Knoxall, to emerge on the pavement on the other side as an apparent member of Sammy Davies' invited guests.

For the whole night I quaffed the best champagne, ate the most expensive and delicious food, and listened in to the chat. And not once was I challenged.

The Astor Club and Le Pigalle were two of the favourite haunts of feared London gangsters such as the Kray Twins and "Mad" Frankie Fraser. I met the twins and Frank. My old boss Vince Landa's right-hand man Ray Thubron, the former pitman who made good in the world of the one-armed bandits, and his brother-in-law John Gaffney, stage-name Johnny Dawn, also spent at least one night in the luxurious and expensive surroundings of Le Pigalle.

Following my hugely successful season in Jersey – successful mainly due to the tutelage of a man who by now had become a very good friend, Ken Wayne – I was signed up to one of the biggest artiste agencies in England, London Management, and worked for two agents, Peter Elliott and Mike Sullivan, two of the biggest names in show-business.

I was becoming a big act, not just in my native North East, and played the Latin Quarter in London, The Lakeside, run by a guy who was a great friend of people in show-business, Bobby Potter, the Circus Tavern and many other clubs in and around the capital, such as Caesars Palace in Luton. I was always given a great reception by the audiences. It seemed I couldn't go wrong.

Although I enjoyed the work in London, I could never settle there. For me, personally, the best thing to come out of London was the Cockney comic Mike Reid (Frank Butcher in Eastenders) who became a very dear friend. In later years Mike managed to get me a speaking part in the hit soap, for which I was very grateful, and it was an interesting experience. But there was so much sitting around, waiting to deliver your line or go on set, I knew it wasn't the life for me.

After London there was tours of the clubs in Scotland, Northern Ireland and Wales, and then back to the north; Manchester, Doncaster, Bradford. I, and the other star acts on the bill, packed them in at The Greaseborough in Rotherham, The Broadway Club in Oldham and all the big clubs in Manchester; The Windsor, The Riverside, The College, The Luxor, The Princess. And wherever I went I met some great characters, many of whom became good friends, and others I knew to steer clear of in future.

In Manchester Jackie Carlton and Al Showman were big names on the club scene, they knew the job inside out and, of course, Bernard Manning opened his own club with the help of his dad, The Embassy. I worked with Bernard a few times and he is a great comedian, but he has never been without his critics for the blue nature of his material, or the racist overtones of some of his gags. In the mid to late '60s and early '70s blue gags became acceptable and these days they are the norm, but some comedians think if they litter their routines with a fuck here and a fuck there that it's funny. Well, often its not, and that is the only way some bad comics can raise a cheap laugh. Martie Caine, God rest her soul, was a case in point. I worked with Marti many times and the lass was a great singer but a mediocre comedienne. Some of her material was distasteful to the point that it never raised a laugh. I told her she should really stick to singing, as she had a great voice.

I am not averse myself to telling blue or what could be labelled racist gags, but the foul language, risqué routines and "racist" one-liners are just part of my act. All it is is comedy; I don't set out to be offensive to anyone, other than hecklers. But the politically correct brigade would say the contrary. That's a pity, because we should all be able to laugh at ourselves, and laugh at one another. What is strange, quirky or funny to the average Asian about the stereotypical English person is as valid in comedy about what the average English person believes is strange, quirky or funny about the stereotypical Asian. There's no offence meant or intended. It's just the comedian connecting with the audience, be it an English audience or an Asian one.

Touring the country, from club to club, was bloody hard work. Many people think a comedian's job is easy, getting up on stage and cracking a few gags for up to an hour might seem an easy way to make a living, but it is bloody hard work. I'd get up on a morning in my digs, phone my agent, ask where I was due next, get packed, jumped in the old Starliner, drive many miles, check into my next guest house, unpack, shower, shave and shit, get dressed, drive off to the next club, do my act, then have a few Bacardi and cokes, maybe go to a nightclub, get back to my digs, crash out, wake up in the morning and telephone my agent to ask where I was going next, pack my bags, drive for many more miles, check into my next digs, unpack, shower, shave and shit, get dressed, drive to the club, do my act, have a few Bacardi and cokes afterwards, then maybe a nightclub, then drive back to my digs and crash out ... there had to be more to life than this.

I enjoyed being up on stage, making people laugh, but everything else associated with it; the driving, the digs, living out of a suitcase, was a pain in the arse. I'd had a taste of the different life, first in Italy and Turkey in my tour of the American service bases, and then in Jersey, where my stage act was almost transformed overnight by Ken Wayne.

Touring the workingmen's clubs my memory would often drift back to my first season in Jersey. I had enjoyed myself. Life was exciting but at the same time more relaxed. I could get out of my hotel room, jump in a lift, walk a few yards and enter the cabaret room. It really was as easy as that, and that was the type of lifestyle for which I yearned.

I had a lot of respect for my fellow North East comedians, like Bobby Thompson, but these people were happy to stay in the North East touring the clubs to earn a living and hardly ever ventured out of the region, never mind the country. Despite my success and my popularity on the North East club circuit, and my strong affiliation with my home-town, I still hankered for another taste of the experiences I had had in Jersey and elsewhere. I wanted to travel, to see more people but, most of all, I wanted to be able to step out of the lift in my hotel room and within minutes step into the cabaret room relaxed enough to do what I did best ... tell gags.

I had stayed in some of the best hotels abroad, and in London, and in some of the dingiest guest houses in England whilst touring the clubs.

A good friend of mine was once travelling to London and he asked if I could recommend a good hotel. I told him of a hotel in Soho where you could go down on a Friday night, get a room, a nice meal and a stunning bird, a full English breakfast on the Saturday morning, another nice evening meal on the night, and another sex-crazed stunner and on the Sunday morning the proprietor would fix him up with a delicious meat sandwich for the long train journey home ... all for £25.50.

"Get away," my mate said. "I don't believe that ... there can't be much meat in the sandwich."

* * * * * * *

The 22-inch aneurysm that was almost killing me wasn't my first brush with potentially deadly health problems, but it was the worst. When the doctor had given me my odds for survival I thought I had more chance catching Lord Lucan riding Shergar than I had beating the problem and surviving, but I was surviving, getting a little fitter every day.

I had suffered a heart attack about 15 years earlier, all down to my lifestyle and the stress associated with it, according to the doctors. It didn't change me. I still pushed myself to the limits, trying to fit as much into my day as possible. I had always been a one for exerting myself, on stage and off. At the start of my career, singing and dancing in the Rock 'n Roll Boys, I used to jump on to the big mantelpiece in the concert room of the Norfolk Hotel in Sunderland, jump into the air and land on the floor doing the splits. I had to be careful, I know, otherwise I could have ended up with two lumps in my throat. When I took to the stage years later, singing From Russia with Love, I Fly to You as my opening number, I would literally fly on to the stage. I suffered many a broken bone. But the acrobatics – the visual stuff – was all part of my act. I knew that, as a comedian, you could produce a laugh just by the way you looked, the way you stood on stage, or your mannerisms. The trick was to weave those comic moments into the delivery of the gags and when the combination was right, the audience then got the full comedy package.

The days of my acrobatic stage antics seemed a world away as I lay in my hospital bed. But I was being cared for well by the angels, the nurses who dedicated their working lives to helping others. And I was getting fitter.

Chapter Twelve

THE STUNNER

The beauty at the bar was the type of woman so stunning she could literally make your jaw drop. I spotted her immediately when I entered the bar at Pontins holiday camp on the sunshine island of Jersey with my pal Jackie Longstaff.

I had returned to Jersey a star, following my success at packing the crowds in in 1969, and virtually everyone on the island knew my face and everywhere I went people would stop me in the street just to say hello.

The stunner was wearing a low-cut blouse and a mini-skirt and her long raven-black hair flowed the length of her sun-tanned back. I stood for a moment, just looking, just admiring, as she walked from the bar, two drinks in hand, towards her friend sitting at a table.

She carried herself well, poised, elegant, confident, aware that most of the eyes of the men in the room were burning into her luscious body. The woman was sex on legs, and I wanted her.

"I don't think much of yours, Jackie," I said, as I slowly walked over to the young woman's table, conscious that she had spotted me making my move.

"Bloody hell, give it a rest," said Jackie, "you're a married man, for God's sake."

"Hello," I said. "Can I get either of you lovely girls a drink?"

"We've just got one," said the stunner.

"You don't mind if me and my mate join you?" I asked.

"No", said the other girl, both of them giggling.

Jackie turned his attention to the stunner's friend for a few minutes and I turned mine to the stunner. Jackie was due on stage and did not seem that interested anyway in the young woman at the table.

I had chatted up hundreds of women over the years, and had an enviable success rate, but, for some unknown reason, I found myself a little tongue-tied in the presence of this dark-haired beauty whose model-type looks made her stand out from the crowd so much.

"Are you here on holiday?" I asked.

"No," said the stunner. "We're working here."

"I thought as much. You're in one of the shows, aren't you, a dancer, maybe?"

"No," said the stunner, "we work as waitresses in here and this is our night off."

It seemed she wasn't impressed with my opening gambit, and first impressions count so much, so it appeared I had a bit of a challenge on, trying to break through a barrier that had somehow been erected between us. I thought maybe her aloofness, her unwillingness to let me in, was perhaps part of her character make-up. Or, perhaps, she just did-n't fancy me, after all, I've never been a Robert Redford in the attractiveness stakes.

I told her a little bit about myself, without trying to appear boastful, and she listened with interest, but I knew I had yet to click.

The stunner was called Diane and she was from East Ham in London. Her father Bill, a docker, and her mother Minnie had met when they were both on holiday in Blackpool. Diane had had an ordinary upbringing, a bit like me, and her family had known hard times.

After leaving school Diane had spent some time working as a punch-card operator in a local factory and later went to work as a switchboard operator at a fashion wholesalers in London's West End, a firm in Great Portland Street, Oxford Circus. It was there that she got her first break into modelling. One of the models was off and they brought her in to do a fashion show and later the firm paid for her to attend Lucy Clayton's School of Modelling in Bond Street.

"As soon as I clapped eyes on you, I knew you must be a model," I said.

Diane was flattered, but for some reason I felt she was resisting my attempts at wooing her. I was trying my best, cracking some of my best one-liners, putting on the charm, engaging in a little name-dropping about the big stars I had worked with. Diane laughed and seemed impressed, but there was something not right, something that was niggling away at my chances of breaking through this beautiful young woman's resolve.

Diane's modelling career hadn't taken off and she and her friend Janet Coughland had become sick of the day-to-day drudgery of working life in London. The young women had decided one Saturday night just to pack their bags and head for Jersey, in the hope they would find work on the island.

On stage Jackie went through his spot, singing some beautiful ballads and other songs popular at the time, with his usual finesse and professionalism. The man was an artist with one of the best singing voices I had ever heard.

Diane was proving a tough nut to crack, but I persevered. I knew there and then that I didn't just want Diane for a quick one-night stand, I wanted her to be my woman. If I was able to get her into bed that night, all well and good, but I knew she was not going to be among one of the hundreds of women I had bedded and said goodbye to the following morning. This woman was something very, very, special.

Then, in an instant, the reason for her impenetrable demeanour became as obvious as my tight-fitting pink suit.

Diane thought I was gay.

I had a lot to thank Ken Wayne for, transforming my image from raw club stand-up comic to cabaret star, but it was within that transformation that the wrong messages could be picked up, and in the current circumstances, trying to woo this stunningly beautiful young woman in front of me, these were signals I could do without.

With my wild, red, highly-coiffeured, shocking head of hair, my pink, expensively-tailored suit with a glitter-edged waistcoat and my Cuban heeled boots, it was no wonder Diane thought I was homosexual. Add to that my stage make-up and the last thought on her mind would be that I was trying to get into her knickers.

"I'm so sorry," said Diane. "I honestly thought you were gay."

"I'm not offended, love," I said.

With that little barrier out of the way, the game was well and truly on. This woman had made such a huge impact on my soul, I would have gladly packed in my job and walked from John O'Groats to Lands End just to be able to share her company. We had only spent a couple of hours together and, like a lovesick teenager, I was absolutely besotted.

With my earlier success on Jersey, the warmest and sunniest of all the Channel Islands, and with me having been voted top comedian in the North of England the previous year, and Top Personality in Jersey, I could by now command quite big fees, earning enough cash to rent a nice bungalow on the island, next to a bungalow owned by Roger Moore. The truth was, the bosses wanted me out of the hotel because of the number of fights I got myself into. Many people visited the bungalow. I had some pulling power and felt like the main man.

Frank Thomasson had bought the West Park Pavilion on the island the previous year and he gutted the place, creating a sunken stage on which the performers would rise up to entertain an audience of about 1,000 or more people.

The show I was starring in in the theatre's Islander Room was simply called Startime 1970 and fellow North East comedian Bobby Pattinson was also on the bill. Singing star Stuart Gillies was among the cast, along with the Ken Wayne's Dolly Birds, a group of talented dancers who shone under the light of Ken's stage directions. The dancers, all attractive young women, included Hazel Lawson, who was principal dancer, Gillian Martin, Carol Eatock, Janice Peeling, Mary Privette, Janet Thomas, Pippa Richards and Elaine Berry. Frank Thomasson, who became a good friend, produced the show, and it was directed by another man who became a good friend of mine, Dick Ray. It was an absolute sell-out.

One of the highlights of the show was when a gold-coloured car entered the stage with myself and the rest of the cast playing the parts of the Beverley Hillbillies. It was an impressive sight and one that Ken Wayne insisted must be included in the performance. There was some difficulty getting the motor into the theatre, but they managed, somehow.

Peter Elliott, of the London Management team, was putting on an Old Time Music Hall show on the island and was having difficulty getting it right. He needed a decent singer and, as Jackie Longstaff was on the island with me, albeit on holiday, I suggested he auditioned for the show. Jackie had to learn 14 songs within one day and ended up writing some of the words on the cuffs of his shirt. He went down a storm and got the job.

There were some familiar faces on the island. My old pal and minder Dennis Davies, former minder to Vince Landa, managed to secure himself a job as an assistant manager at one of the hotels and Ronnie Prenelle, who ran an artiste's agency in the North East, was on the island having just opened a jeweller's shop. Ronnie was really on the run from heavies in the North East who were out to get him for some reason.

I was packing out the West Park Pavilion and earning more than £150 a week. The bungalow was only a few minutes drive from the venue, I was at the height of my popularity and, it seemed, life could not have been better. I became friendly with a millionaire called Ronnie Renald and he would take me to the races in his private aircraft, bung me a wad of notes to gamble, then invited me and a few other stars to his mansion for Sunday lunch. His guests included Vince Hill, Dukes and Lee, and many other star names. After dinner the invited men would be given cigars, their women boxes of the most expensive chocolates, and everyone would quaff the finest champagne. For a barrow boy from Sunderland's East End, this was a life of luxury.

During the week Jackie and I would be performing every day and at the weekend we would go to either Pontins or Butlins, alternating between the two, Jackie singing and me doing my stand-up routine. We both socialised with Fred Pontin and Billy Butlin who, despite their business rivalries, were good friends.

The only thing lacking in my life was the beautiful woman I had seen at the bar in Pontins. After that first night I just couldn't get her out of my head. She occupied most of my thoughts. I just couldn't shake her from my mind. I drove up to the Pontins camp the next day to see her, and we chatted, and from then on I pursued her relentlessly. For four whole weeks I chased her around the island like a man possessed.

A Sunday night arrived and I met up with Diane to take her for a drink in one of the local bars. Perhaps alcohol, I thought, would loosen her up a bit, make her a little more receptive to my undoubted charms. The trouble was, she didn't want to drink alcohol, only soft drinks. I had a quiet word with the barman and persuaded Diane that the aniseed in her drink was just a type of non-alcoholic flavouring. She drank almost half a bottle of Pernod and was absolutely legless. It was an opportunity I couldn't afford to miss.

At the end of the night I persuaded Diane to come back with me to the bungalow, just for a chat and another drink, and she agreed. But when I made my move she ran to the bathroom, locked herself in, and, sitting with her back to the side of the bath panel, firmly pressed her feet on to the door.

"I knew what you were after all along," she said.

It took some time for Diane and I to really get together, but when we did I knew this was one union I wanted to last forever. I was married, with children, Stephen, Phillip, Michelle and Melanie, who were all great kids, and felt guilty about that, and it was something that preyed on Diane's mind and mine. But I knew that my wife, Margaret, who got called Peggy, and I had grown apart, mainly because of the time I had been spending working and, particularly, working abroad. When the time came, if Diane and I were to be together, we would have to face the music, however unpleasant the consequences.

For now, though, we could enjoy our time together, seeing out the last few months of our season in Jersey, enjoying the sunshine and each other's company. We took part in the annual Battle of the Flowers parade, which was judged by Harry H Corbett, of Steptoe & Son fame, the show at The Pavilion packed the crowds in night after night, and earned our bosses plenty of money, and Diane and I finally hit it off. In the end she wanted me as much as I wanted her.

To top it all, I was voted the Best Comedian on the Island, and knew that my time spent in Jersey was time well-spent and would help me further my career in show-business.

* * * * * * *

I could feel the warm lips on my cheek, lying in bed semi-conscious, and opened my eyes slowly but did not find my lovely wife Diane standing at my bedside.

"You raving fucking puff," I said, as Sammy Doran stood there with a bunch of grapes and a wide grin on his face. "You'll get yourself talked about."

"Hello, yer daft old get, how are yee getting on?" He asked.

"I'm all right, kid. I'm all right. You know what it's like. One day you're getting fitter, feel you can do anything, but your body lets you down."

"I woodna worry," said Sammy. "I've nee doubt you'll be up and ouuta here before lang."

I had often wondered why Sammy, who runs The Burton House pub in Sunderland city centre, never lost his Scottish brogue, despite him having lived in the North East for more than 25 years.

Sammy, originally from the Bells Hill area of Glasgow, had worked in the pub and hotel trade since he was a teenager, and knew the business inside out. He started with British Transport Hotels, first working in Gleneagles, and moved to the Royal Station Hotel in Newcastle in the mid 1960s as a cocktail barman, and became a regular face on the city's nightclub scene, hanging around with one of my old friends, Bill Thompson, Vince Landa's accountant, who introduced him to the city's Dolce Vita club.

Sammy had been a good friend of mine for more than 20 years and had been in charge of booking the acts for some of the North East's biggest clubs, among them The Cavendish in Newcastle and The Tavern in South Shields. The manageress of The Cavendish, Ella Todd, was one of the rising stars of the Bailey Organisation and when she moved to The Tavern, Sammy moved with her.

The landlord of The Burton House had many claims to fame. At The Cavendish he had the job of arranging the stage lighting for the visiting stars and would give the star of the show a lighting plan before they went on stage. When Bob Monkhouse played The Cavendish and Sammy asked him if he wanted a lighting plan, Bob told him to use initiative.

Sammy spent more than half an hour searching the club for some lighting system called initiative and almost made the star of the show late on stage, until Ella stepped in to put him right.

Harry Secombe, Georgie Fame, Alan Price, Ertha Kitt, Adam Faith and many other top stars had played Sammy's clubs. When Ertha Kitt was on stage, Sammy's role was as a walk-on butler bringing her four glasses of champagne on a silver tray, which she would quickly drink. Sammy told me that's how she got the purr in her voice, it was really Ertha controlling her wind, purring rather than burping, he said.

When Sammy booked me to play The Tavern for a full week, I could earn myself £1,200, and it was the same for other top comedians, such as Bobby Thompson. In those days you could buy a small house for £300, so that indicates the kind of money we were on at the time.

Sammy was part of the regular crowd who would meet up at Bowers Café opposite Newcastle's central railway station for tea or coffee after a night at the clubs.

Sammy also worked for Eve Collins, talent spotting around the clubs. Eve ran the Sign a Star (SaS) Agency, which had an office underneath The Tavern in Shields.

"I thought maybe you'd come in to ask me to do a show," I said.

"You're in nae fit state," said Sammy.

"Well, it hasn't fucking stopped you before," I said.

"I remember when I had a broken leg and a chalk from my ankle to my balls, it didn't stop you from getting me up on stage."

"Aye," said Sammy, "I remember that. You had to sit on a tall stool all night cracking gags, with your leg in plaster sticking oot. You brought the hoose doon."

"That's always been the thing with you, Sammy," I said. "The show must go on."

"Like that time the lights went out in The Tavern."

"Aye, fucking hell. I'd forgotten about that, you tight git. You gave everyone in the front row a fucking torch to shine on me."

Sammy laughed. "Aye," he said. "And they were bloody good spotlights."

"I turned round to one bloke and asked him to turn the torch off. I said, 'what do you think I am, a fucking moth'?"

Sammy was one of many old friends to visit me in hospital. Graham Stephenson, who runs Barnes Car Sales, in Sunderland, Dougie Parker, who owns and runs Parker's Fish Restaurant in the city, and many others lightened the load of the long days during the time I was battling my way back to fitness.

It's in those times of need when you find out who your real friends are. And these, like many others, proved to be true friends.

Chapter Thirteen
INTO AFRICA

As the huge plane lifted off the tarmac, I marvelled at the ingenuity of mankind. Within a few minutes we were thousands of feet in the air and I looked out of the window at the land mass below and thought about Diane, stuck at home in Sunderland facing the aftermath of being the other woman in what had become an acrimonious split from my wife. A few hours ahead of me was Africa, that dark continent I knew so little about, and cash to be made working in some of the top cabaret rooms in the top hotels in Zambia, Rhodesia, South Africa and so many other countries where ex-patriate workers cried out for a taste of familiar home entertainment.

It had all happened so quickly. I persuaded Diane to come and live with me in Sunderland and, after the 1970 Jersey season came to an end, we stayed for a few weeks at Diane's parents house in East Ham, before moving to Sunderland to face the music following our illicit affair. It was a difficult time for everyone involved.

Diane managed to get a job as a saleswoman in a shoe shop in the town centre and we adapted to our new life together. A few days later, with Diane and I living at my mother's house, Miles Knox called me on the telephone and asked me if I was prepared to work in Africa. It was an opportunity I couldn't afford to miss and, in truth, Diane and I needed the cash.

Miles, who was making a good living in Africa, made arrangements to get my flight tickets and accommodation sorted out, and within hours I was on the plane heading for what was another great adventure. The barrow boy from Sunderland's East End was on his travels again.

Miles, the son of a miner who was born in Seaham Harbour, had served his time as a fitter at Vane Tempest Colliery and it was his links with a local football club in the early days of the CIU league that first sparked his involvement in booking acts. He hit on the idea of getting some decent turns on at the football team's social club, the Seaham York House Club, on a Saturday afternoon and, as most clubs didn't book acts that time of the week, he was on to a sure-fire winner. I was big on the club scene at the time, along with Bobby Thompson, Bobby Pattinson, Johnny Duffy and the like, and we all played Miles' club at one time or another.

He went out to Zambia in 1966, the year after the country had gained its independence, working as a fitter in a copper mine and was surprised at how many ex-pats were working in the copper belt around one of the main towns, Luanshyana, and at a big electricity generating plant about 20 miles away. There were about six copper mines in the area and skilled workers were needed to train the locals. The ex-pats, mainly Brits, worked hard shifts during the day, but their nights were empty, devoid of any entertainment. They had cash to spend, but nothing to spend it on, and they were ensconced in a country whose culture they didn't know or understand, in unfamiliar surroundings, with little more to do than work.

South Africa, Rhodesia and Zambia, to an extent, had attracted hundreds of Brits during the 1950s and 1960s who had emigrated to a new life in countries where the air was fresh and clean and the sun always shone. Like Cecil Rhodes before them, whose mission was to expand British territory and capitalise on African countries natural assets, as well as expanding his own personal wealth, the Brits who headed for the promised land were really the last of the great British empire builders. But the British empire was crumbling fast, as the majority black population of African countries demanded independence. The days of the white minority ruling the black majority were numbered.

I never claimed to understand the political nuances of the situation, or the history that had made Africa what it was then, but I felt strongly that apartheid was wrong. Beaches were segregated for whites and non-whites, the whites called blacks "kaffas" and it was virtually unknown for any black entertainer to perform in a club where the clientele was all white, predominantly white European.

Miles Knox transported the skills and contacts he had developed in the North East of England to Zambia; first getting involved with the local football team, then later securing a job as a PR man for the Zambian Football Association. In 1967, when the John Charles 11 went out on a tour of Africa, Miles was given the job of taking the team around the five stadiums where they were playing their games and was given a budget from sponsors, Rothmans of Pall Mall, to organise a big night of entertainment in Lusaka on the night after the final match. He flew in several entertainers from England, mainly from the North East, and it was a great success.

It was this success that prompted Miles to pack in his job at the copper mine and become a full-time agent. He soon had many top acts on his books; Billy J Kramer, the Carl Denver Trio, Marty Wild, The Avons, to name a few. Through his company Knox Cabaret International Promotions, he linked up with all the top agents, including the Beverley Artistes Agency in the North East of England, and London Management, who had many big stars on their books, including Shirley Bassey, Morecambe and Wise, Tommy Cooper, and soon Bobby Knoxall, as well as many big American stars.

Zambia was a whole new ball game for me. A limousine would pick me up from my hotel to take me to the cabaret venue and I would pass some of the most natural terrain in the world, unspoilt by human hands, teeming with all kinds of wildlife.

Miles had had an accident at the pit a few years earlier and a huge lump of flesh had been torn from the rear of his upper right leg, and almost half his right buttock was missing. Between us we dreamt up a story that, whilst in Africa, Miles spotted a young African girl drowning in a river, jumped in and saved her, but had half his arse bitten off by a crocodile in the process. He was, we said, later presented with a bravery award and it made all the local newspapers. It was a story that was believed by many, right up to this day.

Despite the high life, the best hotels, the chauffeur-driven limousines, the receptive audiences, the good money I was earning, and some of the most breathtaking scenery in the world, I was pissed off. I should have been having the time of my life. But I was so depressed it was showing, and Miles noticed it.

In an effort to give me a lift, Miles encouraged a stripper from Mozambique to visit my hotel room. She was absolutely stunning, with a voluptuous, so shaggable, figure. If I hadn't felt so down I would have been humping her immediately in a session that would have lasted all night under the star-dotted African sky. In days gone by the temptation of such exotic sexual delights would have proven irresistible. But I wasn't bothered; the old cock 'o the north was as flaccid as a wet tea bag and raising him from his slumber would have been as difficult as raising the Titanic.

I knew the reason why I felt so listless, so lethargic, so de-motivated and uninspired. I was missing Diane. I was desperate to be near her, longed to embrace her, and felt as though I had let her down badly. She was in my hometown, the town of my ex wife, a woman scorned, and I was thousands of miles away, lying on a bed in the room of a luxury five-star hotel, with a naked black beauty willing, and able, to meet any kind of sexual demand I made. It was a situation many men can only dream about. But me, I couldn't even raise it.

Miles Knox clicked on, and he was surprised, knowing something of my past sexual encounters, how deep my feelings for Diane ran. He also knew that, in my current state, I would be no good on stage. A depressed comedian is as much use as a timid soldier in battle, a dancer with no feet, a female stripper without tits, a boxer without courage, a footballer without flair.

I was soon to move to Rhodesia, for another comedy tour, working for a man I had met many years earlier in London, Peter Hubbard, the man with so many gangland criminal connections it was difficult to fathom out whether or not he had been tainted. Both Miles, and Peter, knew that without Diane I was half a man, half a stand-up comedian. I had met Peter Hubbard a few months earlier in the La Strada club in Sunderland and he remembered me from my days in The Astor in the capital where I compered for a while. I didn't recollect him, but I did remember his wife, a very attractive woman.

Within 24 hours of miles discovering my pissed-off predicament I was on a plane heading back for England with a return ticket in my pocket and a ticket for Diane. The flights were costly, but Miles and Peter knew that with Diane by my side, I would return to Africa with a smile on my face and the smile would boost my act, and the act would attract the punters. It was a nice gesture by Peter and Miles, but it also made good business sense.

In Sunderland I walked into the shoe shop where Diane was seeing to customers and I told her straight. "Let's get out of here," I said. "We're going to Africa."

It was the start of a real globe-trotting career for me, a ten-year period working seasons in Africa, then flying home and working in the clubs I knew so well in the North East. When the compere at the Ivy Leaf Social Club in Hendon introduced me he would say: "And now, an international cabaret star who has just flown in from Africa ... Bobby Knoxall." It was true. I really had just flown in from Africa.

The best part of it all was that now my soon-to-be wife Diane was travelling with me, and I was determined that wherever I went, she would be sharing my life. We kept our house as a base in Sunderland and for the next ten years would spend much of our time living out of suitcases in some of the best hotels in the world. We would be living like millionaires, eating the best food, drinking the best wine, being chauffeured around in a limousine virtually everywhere we went. For me, it was like winning the pools.

*　*　*　*　*　*　*

The get-well cards were arriving in their scores, some from people I had never heard of or met, and the telephone in the ward was always ringing, mainly people ringing up to see how I was and others who wanted to have a chat. I had just received a call from a man who I worked for in the late 1960s, Colin Noble, a self-made millionaire who built up an empire in the North East, with a string of amusement arcades and other business ventures. Colin was big in the Showman's Guild, and ran fairground attractions and was always one of the first to dip his hand in his pocket and contribute if I was staging a charity show. As well as being very generous, Colin was a great man to work for. I never considered him my boss, more of a mate, really, and we had some great times together.

It was those times we had chatted about on the telephone and it brought back a flood of memories for me.

I got to know Colin when he asked me to do a few shows at the Carousel Club in Chester-le-Street, which was a bit of a knocking shop. It had a good band, led by bass player George Foster, and I compered a few shows. One Christmas time Colin brought in a load of watches and asked me to sell them, some were in good working order and some of them were dodgy. I managed to sell all the good ones and left him with the dodgy watches; it was supposed to be the other way round.

Colin was associated with a man called Liddle Towers, who asked me to meet him one day in Park Lane, Sunderland. I had never met the guy before, so I asked how I would recognise him. He said he had a glass eye. I asked him how I would know which one of his eyes was the glass one, and Liddle said it was the one with the glint of human kindness in it. Liddle had also worked for Vince Landa.

Liddle's nephew, also called Liddle Towers, worked the doors for Colin at the Carousel, and I had many conversations with the young lad, who was as tough as they come. Liddle the younger was a boxing coach and very well known around the Chester-le-Street area. His death, in police custody, after he was restrained by police arresting him outside the Key Club in Birtley was a tragedy. Several police officers restrained him in the car park of the club and bundled him into a police van, but Liddle put up a struggle. He suffered a number of injuries and there was a public outcry, a type of "justice" committee was set up and there were calls for a public inquiry. Eventually, at an inquest in Bishop Auckland, County Durham, a jury returned a verdict of death by misadventure. The campaign group folded, and there never was a public inquiry. But his death in custody still led to claims of police brutality and North East punk rock band, the Angelic Upstarts, brought out a song about the case.

I was working abroad when his death happened, but came back and saw the grief suffered by many who knew him.

Chapter Fourteen
OUT OF AFRICA

The television cameras were beaming my mug all across the African continent when I was compering the Miss South Africa beauty pageant. In the audience were the top business people from Rhodesia, South Africa and Zambia, top government officials, including the Prime Minister of Rhodesia Ian Smith. These were top VIPs, the televised show was being watched by millions and Bobby Knoxall was in his element.

"Do we have anyone in the audience called Smith?" I asked.

Rhodesia's top man raised his hand.

"Your crisps have arrived, Mr Smith," I said.

The fact that I was on prime-time television was not something new to me, I did regular TV shows in Africa and at one time had a mini-series running, The Bobby Knoxall Show. I was on the radio virtually every day, often twice a day, and thousands of people driving to work, then driving back home from work, would hear me crack a few gags or tell a few funny stories. When the canned laughter started, after a few seconds, I would say "Cease!", to cut it, and the word became my catchphrase. Translated it was supposed to mean something rude, but I never fathomed that one out. In the streets I would be recognised everywhere I went and people would shout out "Cease!", "Cease!".

After nine months or so in Zambia, working for Miles Knox, and my agents Peter Elliott and Mike Sullivan, I moved down to Rhodesia and worked for Peter Hubbard and Tony Isaacs. Our team's base was The Celebrity Club in Salisbury, where the resident band was The Vince Clayton Trio (the line-up included Miles Knox's partner Kerry James) and we also had La Boheime, Brett's Nightclub and the place where I really made a name for myself, the Crazy Horse cabaret room in the Beach Hotel in Durban. In Bulaweo there was a sister club to La Boheime, run by a chap called Kerry Le Strange, who brought some of the top acts over from America, including Guy Mitchell and Brooke Benton, the man I had worked with many years earlier touring the American army bases in Italy.

My hotel room was first class, overlooking the beach, and Diane and I could take advantage of any of the facilities, the swimming pool, Jacuzzi, etc, and Diane, being the sun-worshipper that she is, adored the place.

I had never made it as big in England, but, then again, I had never wanted to make it as big there. Africa was a different way of life entirely, Diane and I were living like royalty, and we really had never had it so good.

The acts would do 12 weeks or so in Zambia, then move on to spend a few weeks in Rhodesia, Pretoria, Johannesburg, Port Elizabeth, Capetown and Durban. And there were some top acts working the clubs and hotels; Marty Wilde, Rose Marie, Kiki Dee, strongman Tony Brutus, who became a good friend of mine, Percy Sledge, Billy J Kramer. Diane and I often looked after Marty Wilde's young daughter, Kim, who went on to become a top pop star.

To work in Africa entertainers first had to go before a panel of local big-wigs, a type of censorship panel, whose members would judge whether or not your act was suitable. With my background working in Jersey, there was never any problem and I cleared that first hurdle with flying colours.

One of the first jobs I did, one hour after landing in Rhodesia, was performing in a club where the previous comic had done a runner. I was whisked from the airport by Peter Hubbard and driven to the venue at speed. Despite being jet-lagged after a plane journey lasting several hours, I brought the house down in the club.

Later, in Salisbury, I compered a show in front of a 10,000-strong audience of mainly blacks, in an open-air theatre with Marty Wilde, Kiki Dee, Karl Denver and Tony Brutus among the acts on the bill. There was a cover charge equivalent to about £2 and it was like a madhouse. Most of the audience could not understand a word of English, but they seemed to enjoy themselves and a great deal of money was raised for a charitable cause in the process, a local orphanage for under-privileged children.

Frank Parkington, from Blackburn, Lancashire, was the boss of the Beach Hotel, where Diane and I stayed, and he put me in charge of the cabaret, The Bobby Knoxall Show, which sold out weeks in advance. Banners were put up at the front of the hotel and a cardboard cut-out of yours truly stood at the entrance to the Crazy Horse cabaret room.

One of the speciality acts I brought over was the Mighty Atom, Little Mo, who found fame leading the Roly Polys on the televised Les Dawson show. Mo, a tiny woman who weighed about 20 stone, had the audience in stitches, dancing on her toes on top of a table and performing a mock striptease. Another act I brought over was a top impressionist from Ireland, Bobby Denver, who I had earlier worked with on the North East club scene. Bobby met a girl called Coco and married her.

Apartheid was strict in many African countries but more relaxed in others and it took some time for black entertainers to be accepted in some of the clubs. Johnny Mathis came out there to work and I met him and asked him to come and see my show at the Beach Hotel, leaving instructions for the people on the door to give me a shout when he arrived. Johnny did arrive, but the management wouldn't let him in, just because he was black. I made a scene about this, and even threatened to leave, but it made no difference. That's just the way Africa was.

Miles Knox had managed to bring over a few black acts to play the clubs and hotels, Percy Sledge, Claude Powell, Ertha Kitt, and a talented lady singer I had met many years earlier, Salena Jones, girlfriend of Dennis Stafford, the business partner of bandit empire king Vince Landa, my former boss. At a club in Rhodesia Salena presented me with a top comedy award.

One night she was playing a club where I normally acted as Master of Ceremonies, but this night I was just sticking to my comedy routine, so I asked Tony Brutus, the strongman, to compere, and ran through the lines he needed to say.

I was on stage quite a long time, much to the chagrin of Salena, soaking up the applause and, as always, bringing the house down. Salena was growing impatient and, through her travelling companion Ian Bartell, made it known that if I didn't exit stage left pretty sharpish, she would be on her toes. She didn't have long to wait and Tony Brutus took hold of the mike to announce her on to the stage: "Ladies and gentlemen," he said. "Would you please welcome on stage, American singing sensation Salena Smith." Salena wasn't happy.

Despite my popularity in Africa, the television appearances, the radio show, packing them in at most clubs I played, I still had a bit of fighting edge about me and got into several scrapes, putting a few people in hospital. Living with Diane had calmed me down a lot, but I could still fly off the handle when provoked.

As I was doing so well in the Beach Hotel, Peter Hubbard decided he wanted me to play the bigger club, The Celebrity, in Salisbury, Rhodesia, and it was there that I first met a man I only knew as Karl the German, who was maitre de at the hotel. Now Karl, who was married to a very attractive exotic dancer, got it into his head that I had been shagging his wife. This was, of course, untrue. Karl gave me a load of verbal, so I challenged him to come outside and sort it out. He did, and I hit him so hard he ended up in hospital. He was only a thin fella, who couldn't really handle himself, but the thought of someone giving one to his wife had enraged him so much he suddenly became a hard case.

After that little episode I was due to fly back home anyway for a break, and when I returned to Africa, this time to work at a hotel in Durban, I met the hotel's maitre de – Karl the German. We decided to put our past differences behind us and worked together for many years in Africa, and made ourselves a lot of money.

Miles Knox and I got into a battle with some locals but we had strength on our side, in the form of Tony Brutus. We were all arrested but the chief of police was a big friend of Peter Hubbard and we were freed from the cells without charge.

After ten years on the dark continent, spending about eight months of the year in Zambia, Rhodesia and South Africa, things began to turn ugly. The atmosphere was tense and, quite regularly, Diane and I would hear about whites being murdered on the television news.

On the beach outside our hotel a white guy was gunned down in cold blood. Not so long afterwards, when Diane and our two boys went to a nearby Wimpey Bar for a bite to eat, a tall black man came up to me as I sat on the hotel steps, pointed his finger at me as if his hand was a gun, and said: "White man, we are going to shoot you."

It was a threat I took seriously. Not that I believed that particular guy was going to shoot me dead, but it was symptomatic of what was happening in Africa at that time. The white minority, the last of the great British empire builders, had seen their day and it was obvious things were going to turn very nasty indeed.

One of my bosses, Tony Isaacs, a swarthy-looking, George Raft-type who was always smartly dressed, was killed in a plane crash and it was rumoured that a briefcase full of diamonds went with him. My boss and great friend Peter Hubbard was sacked and went off to find his fortune elsewhere. Alan Goodison, the oner of all the hotels, used all his persuasiveness to try and get me to stay, to take over the booking of the acts for the clubs and hotels. He told me, and then he told Diane separately, that if I stayed and worked for him I would be a millionaire within two years.

But the money didn't interest me. Things had turned sour. Although Diane and I had spent some of the best years of our lives in Rhodesia and South Africa, and our two youngest boys Robert and John spent their earliest years there, we knew it was time to leave.

Peter Hubbard left, then a few days later Diane and I packed our bags, sacked the nannies, said goodbye to the friends we had made, and jumped on a plane to England. After ten years entertaining millions of people, and making it so big on stage, on television and on radio that I had become a household name, it was time to close the door on one of the most successful stages in my career in show-business.

Within a couple of hours, we were out of Africa, and on our arrival in England yet another offer was put to me by a man I worked with many years earlier.

I had been back in England only a few minutes and it appeared my globe-trotting days were far from over.

* * * * * * *

Diane was a pillar of strength, coming to the hospital every day, seeing to our four lads at home, and, all the time giving me the encouragement to fight towards fitness. The lads, and most of my extended family, were regular visitors too.

With so much time on my hands, I had time to reminisce, time to look back on the good times, where I went wrong, the characters I had met and the long-lasting friendships I had formed. What I really wanted to do was plan ahead for the future, but in the midst of so much uncertainty there was nothing concrete to grab hold of, nothing firm I could head towards. My future lay in the hands of the doctors and nurses looking after me and, of course, a lot of it was down to myself, having the will-power to fight the illness, thinking positive even when all hope appeared lost.

"Hello cocker," my sister Violet appeared, clutching a copy of the Sunderland Echo, my regular local newspaper. Slyly, she opened the cabinet by the side of my bed and slipped two 20 packets of Embassy Regal king size inside.

"I shouldn't be doing this," she said. "In your state the last thing you need is fags."

"Shut up, woman," I said. "I get the same nagging day in day out, if not from you then it's the doctors and nurses on my back. For God's sake, can a man not have a smoke in peace."

"It's your funeral," said our Vi.

My sister was a caring lass, just like the rest of them, but sometimes she let her heart rule her head, like the time she fell for a well-known local villain called Stuart Mottram, otherwise known as Benny the Brick, the king of Seaham Harbour and an on-off friend of another of my associates, George Craig, who I had taken under my wing when he was a young boy.

Benny had served time in jail for various scams and had a feared reputation in Sunderland and in Seaham. His wife left him to bring up three kids on his own and Benny did an admirable job. He was not short of women, though, and one of his jail sentences came about after he bedded the wife of a well-known councillor in County Durham, she became the woman scorned, and bricks started flying in all directions. Benny took the full force of the law, and ended up in Durham Jail.

Benny attended many of my shows and, thankfully, when I outlined the story of how he got his name, he took it how it was intended, in good humour.

The story was that he and my sister Violet were walking along Fawcett Street, one of the main shopping streets in Sunderland, in the run-up to Christmas and all the shop windows were full of gifts ready to be bought and packed for loved ones.

The couple passed an electrical shop.

"Eeeh, Benny, look at that," said Vi. "Our youngen would love that hi-fi."

Benny put his hand in his pocket, pulled out a brick, smashed the window, and grabbed the hi-fi.

A little further on, Vi spotted a gleaming Chopper bike in the window of a cycle shop.

"My sister's lad would love that," she said.

Benny picked up a brick, smashed the window, grabbed the bike, and started wheeling it along the street.

"Isn't that sheepskin coat lovely," said Vi, as they passed a clothes shop.

"What do you think it is," said Benny, "do you think I'm fucking made of bricks, or what?"

In truth Stuart Mottram got the nickname Benny because when he was working on the taxis he used a false ID card belonging to a chap called Benjamin. The brick part of the nickname came about after he put the windows out in a car owned by one of his debtors. The man refused to pay the debts so every time the cash didn't arrive on the due date, Benny smashed the windows in his top-of-the range motor. He did it several times, then the money arrived. This straightforward, if unorthodox, method of alerting debtors to the fact that payment was due stayed with him. It was better than paying to send the bailiffs around, and people who owed Benny cash, made sure they paid on time and in full.

Benny also placed bets for me around the bookies, but it was a long time before I found out he was pocketing the cash and hoping that my horse never came in. He must have earned hundreds in his time taking my betting slips to Gus Carter's. But I was the fool there.

Later I managed to secure the licence for the Pennywell Social Club in Pickering Road, Sunderland, and the place could have been a goldmine. My mate Mike Reid came up from London specially to put a show on for me and the place was packed, the beer was flowing freely, and I knew it could be the start of something big.

But things went belly-up. Two lesbians from Seaham came in one night and started heckling, then pulled out baseball bats and laid into me and my wife. It ended up in a court case and they got done. It was all a bit of a mess.

The club could have been a success but, for one reason and another, I lost thousands of pounds on that one business venture alone. It still owes me £20,000 ... but I've been waiting for repayment for years.

After our years in Africa there was talk of me taking over the Eastender Club in Sunderland's East End, and I did have some conversation with my old friend Jimmy Bute about the possibilities, but when I came back the deal had been done and the carpet pulled from under my feet. Perhaps people knew that if Bobby Knoxall was running a club in the East End, where he was born, a hell of a lot of business would have been lost by some other pubs and clubs in the area. And that's not sour grapes, that's a fact.

During my career I had mixed with some of the heaviest villains in the country, and particularly in Sunderland, but I never ended up in jail myself. That's because I had the rare talent of being able to make people laugh and the drive to push ahead in what became a rewarding career.

Had I not had that talent, I know that, just like many of the lads I associated with in Sunderland, Stuart Mottram, George Craig and Dennis Davies just to name three, I would have ended up behind bars.

Chapter Fifteen
THE CUP FINAL

The longed-for final whistle went and Wembley Stadium, the World of Sport television studio I was sitting in, and the whole of Sunderland, erupted with joy. It was Sunderland Football Club's finest hour, and Bobby Knoxall's – as well as thousands of other Sunderland fans' – greatest sporting moment of all time. The manager, Bob Stokoe, ran across the pitch, still wearing his mac and his trilby hat, and embraced goalkeeper Jimmy Montgomery in a scene that would be repeated thousands of times over on television screens across Wearside for years to come.

Ian Porterfield got the goal that counted and Jimmy Montgomery carried out the most acrobatic double-save I had ever seen. As the Little General, Bobby Kerr, whom I had known since he was only 16, lifted the FA Cup, Wembley Stadium was a sea of red and white and the Roker Roar reverberated around the stands. Never before had such a roar been heard around the twin towers. The sweet smell of victory was doubly delightful because all the critics thought it couldn't be done; lowly Sunderland AFC, Second Division lightweights taking on the mighty high-flying First Division giants Leeds United in the greatest football competition in the world. The bookies had Leeds firm favourites. Some bookies put the odds for Sunderland at a staggering 250-1. Many Sunderland fans scored in more ways than one on that glorious day.

More than 25,000 Sunderland fans made the long trip to London, meeting thousands more at Wembley, and Sunderland became a ghost town for the day, at least after 12 noon. The only people in the windy Market Square were those without televisions at home watching the match in the TV shop windows.

In London I recognised so many faces it was as if the town had been relocated to the capital for the day. I was so well-known in my home-town literally hundreds of people acknowledged me on the London streets, all with beaming smiles, enjoying the town's moment of national glory.

When the match started there was one almighty roar from the majority of the Sunderland contingent and the most tense 90 minutes of football I had ever sat through was about to begin.

Don Revie led the "invincible" Leeds United team on to the hallowed turf dressed in a smart suit, and Bob Stokoe led my team out, the underdogs, dressed in a tracksuit. Montgomery, Malone, Guthrie, Horswill, Watson, Pitt, Kerr, Hughes, Halom, Porterfield, Tueart and substitute Young. The names of these footballers would be etched on the minds of Sunderland fans for years to come.

Most of the Press photographers stood behind Jimmy Montgomery's goal, obviously expecting all the action at that end, having followed the critics, the sporting pundits and the bookies odds, and a solitary figure, Jack Carroll, a photographer from the Sunderland Echo, stood behind the goal occupied by the Leeds goalkeeper.

Only one photographer really captured the golden moment when the one crucial goal was scored, and that was Jack, and it was a photograph that blessed the front page of that night's Sunderland Football Echo under the simple, straightforward, and proud headline "They've Done It!"

The game wasn't the greatest feast of football I had ever seen, nor was it that entertaining when it came to footballing skills or on-the-pitch strategy, but the tension was almost tangible, the emotion raw, and the passion of the fans for real.

The know-it-all football pundits passed patronising comments about Sunderland's chances, and if they could not think of a patronising comment, they thought of something condescending instead. The footballing "experts" were about to eat their words, but being a Sunderland lad, I did not intend to rub it in. I was too busy enjoying the moment.

I had been sitting alongside Frank Carson in the television studio at Wembley and, of course, I said Sunderland would win. Frank cracked a few gags – it was the way he told them – and I cracked a few. Frank said he believed Leeds would win and he and I shook hands on a bit of a wager.

I sat alone directly behind the Queen and longed to be amongst my people; the people of Sunderland, whose spirit and passion overwhelmed the travelling Leeds contingent.

I had been down to the lads' dressing room before the match, boosting them up with a few jokes and banter, trying to ease the tension a little bit, and after the match I was straight back down to the dressing room again where the players were going daft. They, and the fans, were deliriously happy.

Sunderland AFC's FA Cup run in 1973 took me out of Africa for a spell, and my agent Peter Hubbard was pulling his hair out. "I've got thousands of people here waiting to see your act," he said. "You're topping the bill for fuck sake."

I told Peter straight, I wasn't returning to Africa until Sunderland's cup run was over, and most fans believed it would be over once we reached the latter stages playing against the likes of Manchester City and Arsenal. I had been a Sunderland fan all my life and I wasn't about to miss out on what was developing into their best FA Cup run since 1937.

The whole town got behind the lads in a big way. The streets were lined with red and white bunting, the shops were full of scarves, rosettes and all kinds of red and white merchandise imaginable and some girls started wearing red and white knickers, flashing them in public.

Bobby Knoxall joined the team to launch a record, Sunderland All The Way, which had the financial backing of my good friend Colin Noble and George Foster, the man who looked after Chubby Brown. The 45rpm single made it into the top 40 nationally (just) and it was the best-selling single on Wearside.

It had a catchy chorus:

> *Sunderland will be in the First Division*
> *Scoring goals in every game they play*
> *Sunderland will be in the First Division*
> *It's going to be red and white all the way*

Back in Africa Peter Hubbard was hoping Sunderland would get knocked out, so that I could return to work and earn him and I a few quid. But it wasn't to be and when Sunderland secured a cup tie against Arsenal, Peter, a lifelong Arsenal fan and shareholder, decided he would bail out of Africa, too. He came to Sunderland and stayed at the Seaburn Hotel.

Tickets for the Wembley final were like goal-dust and, for some reason, everyone in the town thought Bobby Knoxall had a boat-load. My telephone never stopped ringing with people calling who I had never heard of, begging me, pleading with me, for tickets. I only had ONE ticket, given to me by Billy Hughes, and I wasn't about to sell it or give it away.

There was a promoter cum agent type who had slack hand-fulls of tickets, who also did deals for the players, getting them new cars and the like, but the only thing he had to do with me was promoting the record. He got himself into a little bother.

A few days before the final I travelled south with the team and the coach broke down. I spent several hours cracking jokes to keep the lads' spirits up. We were heading to Rod Stewart's mansion house in the Hereford countryside. I had met Rod before, when music promoter Geoff Docherty brought him up to the Mecca nightclub in Sunderland. Rod, who is a true football fan, treated us well with his hospitality, lovely food, fine wine. We played snooker and Rod gave Billy Hughes, one of the team's star players, a gold disc and dished LPs out to several of the others.

On the great day itself I was staying in the Regent's Palace Hotel, as was my great friend Peter Hubbard and at breakfast time, just a few hours before kick-off, I spotted a few familiar faces at the breakfast tables. They were all Sunderland villains who had travelled down to London without tickets, hitching lifts, and sleeping rough overnight, just for the chance to be there, soaking up the atmosphere.

The villains hadn't booked into the hotel, but ordered breakfast, and, after they had scoffed cereal, the full English, a round of toast, and drank pots of tea and coffee, the waitress asked each for their room numbers and they just plucked a number from the air. "Room sixty three," said one, in a put-on posh accent. "Room one o five", said another. When the waitress's back was turned they were up and away. I was asked if I knew any of the lads. "Never seen them before in my life," I said.

After the match there was a big party in a London hotel for the players, with Suzie Quatro and Frankie Vaughan making guest appearances. I went along with Peter, and the players were out of their heads. Afterwards we joined Colin Noble and George Foster to go to The Talk of the Town where Matt Munro, a good friend of mine, was performing.

After the big day, Peter and I flew out to Rhodesia on the Sunday, and we missed all the big celebrations. I would have loved to have been at the La Strada, where a huge party was planned the following week for the players, and in Sunderland when the fans greeted the team on their victory parade. The whole of Sunderland turned out to greet the players, tens upon tens of thousands lining the parade route from the town's border with Durham City right down to the gates of Roker Park. A sea of jubilant faces amongst a sea of red and white. The open-topped coach moved off from Carrville, on the outskirts of Durham City at about 7pm on the Tuesday after the Wembley final and there were such huge crowds, the players did not arrive at Roker Park until well over two hours later.

Sunderland had never seen anything like it before, street parties were held all over the town, going on well into the early hours of the morning. There was such a huge lift in the town, I was told, that you could almost feel it.

From then on, for Bob Stokoe and his men, the only way was up. I felt privileged to have played a small part in the great day, and in the build-up to it. It was the most memorable sporting day of my life, and the most abiding footballing memory for me and for thousands of others.

* * * * * * *

I was eating. It was only rice pudding, but I was eating, and that proved I was getting back on the road to fitness. For the first few days since my life-saving operation I had only been drinking tea and lemonade, gallons and gallons of it, but you can't survive on fluids alone, and the first semi-solids entering my guts was an encouraging sign. The physiotherapy was working well, too, and for the first time I was able to walk unaided, out of the wheelchair, free of the walking frame, and back on old Shanks's pony.

Diane had even noticed a change in my mental state. We could actually have a normal conversation without me spouting gibberish, as if I was showing the signs of senile dementia or alzheimer's disease. I still had some way to go, but the doctors were pleased with my progress and were talking about me being able to go home within the new few days. That was something I was looking forward to immensely.

Lying in a hospital bed without little more to do than think, made me very aware of how much I had taken things for granted over the years. Just being able to walk, independently, just standing on your own two feet and putting one foot in front of the other was marvellous for me. But there were thousands of people who would never be able to do that through disability or infirmity.

A few of the people in the hospital beds would never see the outside world again, their illnesses were so serious. Most were old, who we would say had had a good innings, but some were only middle-aged and others just out of their teenage years. It was so sad, seeing them deteriorate and knowing that their days were numbered.

My experience and my latest operation had brought about a change in me. I was not afraid of death. But I had so much I still wanted to do, I knew I had to remain positive in spirit and plan for the future.

I wanted to get back on stage. I wanted to do more charity shows for some of the people who were worse off than myself. I also wanted to earn money, not for me, but for me to leave to Diane and the boys when I finally popped my clogs, kicked the bucket, went to meet all the old comics at that great stage in the sky.

I often boasted that I had made at least two million pounds during my career and that I had blown the lot, on booze, cigarettes, women and gambling. But when I said that, it was for comic effect, just to raise a laugh. In truth it wasn't something I was particularly proud of.

What I wanted to do was get back to work and I decided there were two other things I wanted to do before I die. One was to write my life story, the small profits from which would go to my wife and sons, and the second was to produce my first video, for the same reason. Other comics had done several videos, but I had yet to do one.

As soon as I got home, I decided, I would make plans, contact the people I needed to, and press ahead.

The book (this book) and the video would be my legacy to my family and would, hopefully, remind my hundreds of fans about some of the great times we had.

Chapter Sixteen
THE COMEDIANS

There were two toilets in Tommy Cooper's mansion-style house in Buckinghamshire, but they appeared to be permanently engaged, and there was so much drink flowing at the party everyone was bursting for a pee. Some of the top agents in showbiz had been invited along with many top stars, Roger Moore, Dorothy Squires, my old boss Peter Elliott were among them. In one of the loos a man was standing having a slash, and in the other there was a woman sitting on the nettie. Whenever anyone tried either lavatory, there was someone in.

Tommy pulled back the blinds on the large windows overlooking his garden, switched on the bright security lights, and declared: "The lawn's getting a good watering tonight."

In the bushes women were crouched down, their knickers around their ankles, and several men were lined up at the edge of the lawn relieving themselves. Tommy was almost in tears, his shoulders moving up and down to the rhythm of his hearty, raucous, laugh, as they always did.

The chap having a run-off in one of the loos, he revealed, and the lady in the other loo, were mannequins, all dressed up and strategically positioned to give the impression they were real people on the toilet. It was a classic Cooper joke played on his invited guests, and it was the type of thing Tommy did for a laugh.

I had met Tommy Cooper, one of the greatest British comics of all time, several times over the years. I was surprised to learn that he had a twin brother, who ran a magic shop somewhere in London.

Tommy was playing The Fiesta club in Stockton and took ill one night and I was asked to fill in. The thought of me doing the show for a man who was a British comic institution didn't just worry me ... I was bloody petrified. Everyone coming into the club, one of the biggest in the North East, would be expecting the big man himself, and they would have to do with me. I had never felt so nervous, but I didn't reach for the bottle, it was always a strict rule of mine that I never drank alcohol before going on stage or during my act, but always made up for it afterwards.

Tommy sat in the audience during the show – which I found just as unnerving – and he liked it. So much so that he took another night off, with me filling in for him again. The audience were great to me, absolutely marvellous, and my two nights filling in for Tommy Cooper earned me a booking in my own name at The Fiesta, topping the bill the following month.

Tommy was one of the comics I most admired but there were others who I would rate alongside him, Bob Monkhouse, who fears no one, and Ken Dodd, that great Liverpudlian who has become a national treasure. Bob Monkhouse wrote gags for the recently departed Bob Hope, a comic I most admired in my younger days when I was hoping to enter the business.

One top comedian, whom I shall not name to spare him his blushes, promised to get me a part in a 13-week television series on one condition; I allowed him to go to bed with my wife Diane. I turned him down, of course.

I spent a week at The Broadway Club in Oldham with another top comedian, Frankie Howerd, whose dressing room was next to the band. Frankie used to carry an old-fashioned record player around with him, to listen to music in his room, and usually kept himself to himself. This week I was opening the show and acting as MC, and Frankie was doing the second spot. Every night, for the full week, Frankie would go into his dressing room and play the single Ghost-riders in the Sky at full blast, over and over again. His room would almost shake and members of the band were naturally pissed off, but didn't say anything to him; Frankie was a big star. Frankie said little to me during the week, and even less to the band, but on the night he left Oldham, after his final spot on stage, he called into the band's dressing room and asked: "Do any of you lads know the words to Ghost-riders in the Sky? Frankie must have thought that was hilarious, but the band didn't see the funny side.

In a career in comedy, like in any other career, when opportunity knocks you grab it, and two came my way within a year of each other; one was a chance to appear in that hugely successful series The

172

Comedians, and the other was at shot at Opportunity Knocks, with Hughie Green.

I was working in Africa when the Comedians opportunity arose and Bob Deplidge, who was by then my manager, encouraged me to give it my best shot. I travelled back to England and went down to the television recording studios in Manchester with Bob, Bill Reeves, and Diane, and all the regular stand-ups were there.

Most of the other comics stood up on stage and did about ten or 15 minutes worth of gags, but I was on stage for an hour. Later, in the green room, I asked Jim Bowen, one of The Comedians who later had a huge television hit series with Bullseye, what the score was. He told me the producers were showing all the other comedians my tape. Basically, they were nicking all my gags, and there was plenty of material for them to share. Whenever anyone asks me if I starred in The Comedians I say, no I didn't, but my gags did. I did get a mention in the book of the same name, so that was some consolation. I wasn't really that bothered about it, anyway, and wanted to get back to Africa. I was asked to appear later on the spin-off Wheeltappers and Shunters Social Club and in The Comedians show in Blackpool and London but, again, it just wasn't my cup of tea. There was little I could do about having my gags nicked, there's no copyright in gags, and people have been doing it for years.

A similar thing happened to my old Jersey sparring partner Alan Fox, from South Shields. He was in a summer season on the Isle of Man at the time, travelled over to Manchester, did his spot and was paid to appear in ten of The Comedians shows, but ended up appearing in only three and that, he says, was just a token gesture by the producers of the programme. They were using us as more or less scriptwriters for the bigger names.

My Opportunity Knocks appearance, like The Comedians, became a non-appearance, despite me getting more than 100 on the old clapometer. The audience loved me, but, for whatever reason, Hughie Green did not. Again the filming took place in the studios in Manchester. I didn't hang around and was soon off to one of my summer seasons in Jersey. In the North East we did have Tyne Tees Television, based in Newcastle, but, sadly, it was never used as good as it could have been as a platform for talent in the region. I did star in a video, North East Comedy Classics, produced by Tyne Tees, along with Bobby Thompson and a few other North East comedians, and it sold very well.

The North East has always been renowned for producing good comedians, and several of us had shots at starring in The Comedians show. Although mine was a non-appearance on the television, I did travel to the Far East doing the show with my great friend Mike Reid and fellow comedian Pat Mooney.

I first met Mike Reid in a place called Nelson, a mountainous area in South Wales, in the late 1960s when Jackie Longstaff and I were doing a Sunday afternoon show in one of the local clubs. Mike Reid was there as a mime act. After our stage acts we drove off, Jackie and I in my impressive sky-blue American Starliner, up and down the mountains, and when we arrived at a local shop Mike Reid was there trying to buy some tobacco, which the shop didn't have.

Mike and I got cracking on, he said he was impressed by my motor, and I suggested he followed Jackie and I along to another shop where they would sell his baccy. During our week or so in South Wales Mike and I became friendly, and we promised to keep in touch with each other.

At the time of The Comedians auditions, Mike rang me up to say he was in with a chance and I gave him just one piece of advice – do not do more than ten or 15 minutes. He did a slot of about 15 minutes and became one of the stars of the hit series. I always knew he had the talent and the drive to succeed. He was always a brilliant comedian, but far more popular in his native London than he ever was in the North of England, but that was to be expected.

I don't know why Mike and I hit it off so well. Perhaps it was because he and I were so street-wise and came from similar backgrounds, but were brought up at different ends of the country. Mike introduced me to The Krays and Frankie Fraser, whom he knew quite well, but I had already met these guys during my days in The Astor Club.

On our Comedians tour in the Far East, Mike once asked me why I always put my suitcases in the baggage area of the plane, like everyone else, but always carried my stage suits with me, unlike other people. "That's facking strange that," he would say.

I told him that's what I had been trained to do.

When we arrived in Bombay we only had two-and-a-half hours before we were on stage and, unluckily, all our suitcases had gone on to another destination. Mike Reid stood there in a pair of slacks and a T shirt with some Cockney slogan on the front and Pat Mooney was dressed in a pair of old jeans and was also wearing a T shirt: "What the fack are we going to do?" Asked Mike.

When we arrived at the big hotel for our act, Mike and Pat Mooney looked like two raggy-arsed tourists, but Bobby Knoxall looked impeccably smart, in his neatly-tailored, bright, clean, stage suit. I was ready for the show.

"You know earlier when you asked me why I always carry my suits?" I asked Mike.

"Yeah."

I looked him and Pat Mooney up and down, as condescendingly as possible.

"That's why," I said.

"Facking smart arse," said Mike.

My path, and that of Mike Reid, would pass again several times and, despite his huge rise to television fame, he never forgot Bobby Knoxall and, as he had promised, he stayed in touch.

*   *   *   *   *   *   *

"Best of luck to you Bobby," the ambulance driver said as he pulled up outside our three-bedroomed council house on the Farringdon estate in Sunderland.

"Thanks, son," I said and Diane was soon helping me out of the back of the ambulance and into our small semi-detached house. Wherever I had travelled, the Far East, the Middle East, Africa the Channel Islands and across the British Isles, I always got the same feeling when I entered our house. There really isn't any place like home.

The sitting room was packed out with my friends and relations, and some of Diane's family, and our four boys were there, John, Robert, Ryan and Brent, all happy to see me coming through the door. My old mate Jackie Longstaff sat in one of the armchairs, puffing away on an Embassy Regal king size, and John Sawyer, a great family friend from London, was also in the house.

"Welcome home Bobby, son," said Jackie.

"It's great to see you," said John.

All the armchairs, and most of the sitting room floor, were occupied, but in the corner, opposite the television, stood my chair. Today it was the most comfortable armchair I had ever sat in.

The mantelpiece and the window sill were packed with get-well cards. There were cards from the Sunderland manager Peter Reid, the club captain Mickey Gray, the big man Niall Quinn, from Bobby Kerr, Mickey Horswill and other members of the 1973 FA Cup winning team, from older former players like Charlie Hurley and in a frame was a signed tea towel. There was a simple message written on the tea towel. "Thanks for helping us win the FA Cup," it said, and it was from the cup-winning team's manager Bob Stokoe.

Sammy Doran had sent a card – and I didn't even know he could write – and there were messages from Graham Stephenson, Dougie Parker, George Wilson, Geoff Docherty, Tommy Conroy, Adrian Marshall and from many, many people who had supported me over the past 50 years.

Then there were the cards from the comedians and celebrities I had worked with, Frank Carson, Freddie Starr, Mike Reid, my great friend Ken Wayne, were among them.

I sat in my armchair and read as many messages in the cards that I could.

And for a moment, I felt overwhelmed.

I was overwhelmed by the warmth of the messages, the number of get-well cards I had received, and the welcome from my friends and family. These were genuine, caring, people, who showed they cared about me in many different ways.

I was so overwhelmed by this genuine show of affection, my eyes filled with tears. I was the big fella, slumped in my armchair; the big fella who only a couple of weeks ago was at death's door. The big fella who was as hard as nails.

I had come through it. The seven-hour operation that had left a scar across my guts as if I had been slashed from side to side by a dyslexic Zorro, the treatment, the after-care, the physiotherapy, the fighting back after being given survival odds of 70-30 in favour of me dying. I had been beyond the pain barrier, almost stared my maker in the eye, and here I was now, sitting in my own armchair in my house, surrounded by my loving family and friends.

The surgeons at Sunderland General Hospital had saved my life. I had been given a second chance.

"Are you all right, Bobby?" Asked Diane, who could see a tear running down my cheek.

"Never been better, love," I said. "I've never been better."

Top: At the Beach Hotel in Durban, South Africa, I broke all records.

Left: At The Mayfair in Durban, South Africa, I broke wind.

INTO AFRICA

Top: At The Beach Hotel in South Africa there was a cardboard cut-out of yours truly, to advertise my show.

Left: With Karl Gilka, who accused me of shagging his stripper missus.

THE SUMMER OF 69

The cartoon advertising Grin and Tonic, our summer show in Jersey in 1969.

Below: Alan Fox, Dick Wray, impressionist Mike Carter and Ken Wayne.

FAME IN JERSEY

Left: Diane and I in the annual Battle of the Flowers festival.

Left middle: Myself and fellow comedian Alan Fox soak up the Jersey sun.

Bottom: With some of the Jersey show's management team, including Frank Thomasson (on left) and Bob Deplidge (sitting next to me).

WITH THE GORGEOUS KEN WAYNE DANCERS

A FEW ROUNDS

Top: With footballer Alex Rae and boxer John Conteh.

Left: With boxer Chris Finnegan and Irish comic Bal Moan.

Below: With Brendan Ingle, former manager of Prince Naseem, Boxer Junior Whitter, and veteran boxer Tommy Miller.

With two of the biggest hitters of all time. World boxing champion
Ricky Hatton (above) and (below) Ernie Shavers.

Top: At the River Wear Social Club in Hendon Sunderland, filming for my video, due out at the same time as this book.

Left: With television personality Kathy Secker and businessman Matt Roseberry launching Bobby Knoxall's Chuckles for Charity Roadshow 2003. The roadshow, probably my last charity effort, aims to raise thousands of pounds towards building a new hospice for children in Sunderland.

Chapter Seventeen

THE MIDDLE AND FAR EAST

The plane had only touched down 20 minutes earlier and Diane and I were walking through Heathrow Airport when I bumped into a familiar face from the 1960s, Bill Thompson, former manager and accountant for the bandit king Vince Landa, who was now working as an agent taking acts out to the Middle East and the Far East.

Africa had become a dangerous place to live and work and Diane and I, with our boys, had decided to get out before we became part of the crime statistics. I had seen much violence in my life, and had been involved in many scraps myself, but the tension and fear in South Africa was something I had never come across before and was now part of everyday life. The blacks were becoming more demanding and intimidating and white minority rule appeared to be coming to an end. Every day we were hearing about shootings and violent attacks and every day Diane and I knew that our days touring Africa were numbered.

Diane had soaked up so much of the South African sun she looked more black than white when we left the volatile country. At the airport for our flight to England someone called her "kaffa" – the name for an African slave – and ordered her to collect their suitcases.

At Heathrow, when we alighted the aircraft, the English weather hit us hard, but it was good to be back on home soil.

Bill Thompson told me he needed a comic for the Middle East and Far East tours he was organising and he said I would fit the bill perfectly. He was organising acts for Dubai, Abu Dhabi, Bahrain, and Bangkok, Bombay and Hong Kong. I was flattered. There aren't many acts, I thought, who could come off a plane after ten years touring one continent to be asked, only 30 minutes after landing, to jet off to another continent to work. I told Bill I was up for it, but, first, Diane and I needed a break and we had a few things to sort out in Sunderland, not least to get our two boys John and Robert settled at home and school.

Our experiences in Africa had been memorable. We had seen first hand some of the world's most outstanding scenery; we had visited places many people could only ever dream about and had tasted the kind of lifestyle usually reserved for national celebrities or millionaires. But we were just as comfortable at Diane's parents' modest home in East Ham and our own small council house in Sunderland as we were in any five-star hotel.

I was only a few days in England when I got a call from Bill Thompson, as he had promised, who urged me to get a flight out to Hong Kong as soon as possible. He told me he needed me on this tour and he offered me the kind of cash that was hard to turn down. After Diane and the boys had settled back in Sunderland I was off on my international travels again. The barrow boy from Sunderland's East End was destined for the Middle East and the Far East, touring three times a year, for 28 days or 32 days, to work in some of the top hotels and cabaret venues the big cities had to offer and, for which, I would be handsomely rewarded.

Bill Thompson, who had become very well-known on the London agents' circuit, had already had comics Jim Davidson and Billy Connolly out on tours of the Middle East and the Far East. As well as working with my old mates Mike Reid and Pat Mooney, others on the tour included Marti Caine, Marti Wilde and The Searchers. As well as topping the bill as the comic, I was to be the MC for the shows.

Marti Caine, as I explained earlier, tried to be funny but her gags went down like a lead balloon. One centred on the usefulness of the Pope's bollocks. Marti just wasn't funny, so I encouraged her to do what she did best, sing, and when she accepted my advice, the tour went on to be a success. Mike Reid, Pat Mooney and I did a few ten-minute spots in a pub called The Londoner in Dubai, where all the Brits frequented, and the audience was appreciative. There was plenty of clubs to do; Bangers Club, the Rugby Club, the Cricket Club, the Yacht Club, all with ex-patriate British audiences who clamoured for a taste of home.

It was whilst I was out in the Middle East that I took a call for Mike Reid from his agent who told me he had secured a part in Eastenders. Mike was over the moon, scheduled to make a number of appearances, and made such an impression he became a household name as Frank Butcher. He deserved the success.

In my bit part in Eastenders later came my big speaking part in the café in Albert Square. "Two teas, please," I said. "Two teas, please," I said again, when I was finding it difficult to get served. Then I said: "Who do you have to sleep with to get a cup of tea around here?" The lines weren't the best ever heard on Eastenders, but I was grateful to Mike Reid for getting me in there. I was never asked to go back. It really wasn't for me, anyway.

It was during my time in the Middle East that my health really started to suffer. At Diane's parents' home in East Ham, whilst on a break from touring, I had a heart attack in the bath and had treatment in a hospital for five days before I was taken home to Sunderland where I was put under a heart specialist at the general hospital. It was on a later tour with Bill Thompson that it appeared I had suffered a heart attack on stage. That's when Judith Durham helped to get me home.

The tours of the Middle East and Far East were good earners for me and it was great to be able to travel, see different parts of the world and to meet some very interesting people. Had my health not suffered, I could have continued with the tours, but all good things have to come to an end sometime.

My association with Bill Thompson, who was then working for the Theatrical Management Corporation, later led to me meeting one of the biggest movie stars the world has ever known.

I had just finished a tour of Hong Kong and was back at home doing a bit of work in the clubs, when Bill rang me up and asked me how I was, whether or not I had enjoyed Hong Kong, and asked if I could do him a favour by acting as compere at a lunchtime event at The Gosforth Park Hotel in Newcastle.

Now Bill knew that I hated working lunchtimes and had stopped afternoon sessions many years earlier. I had a bit of a moan about it, but told him that, as a special and one-off favour, I would go to Gosforth and do 20 minutes of comedy and introduce the guest speaker. I arranged to meet Bill at about 12.30pm.

At the hotel I had a bit crack on with Bill and then I asked him who the guest speaker was. "He's over there," said Bill, pointing to a tall, smartly-dressed man who had his back to me.

I walked over to the man and said: "Hello, I'm Bobby ..." He turned round and I was so speechless I couldn't tell him my surname.

There, standing in front of me, was Charlton Heston. "Call me Chuck," he said.

The man had such a presence and strength of character I was totally in awe of him. I had seen him in all the epic movies, such as The Ten Commandments and here I was now, talking to one of the greatest movie stars that had ever lived.

I had to think of a good line to introduce him as the guest speaker. But what could I say about such a huge star that could sum up the man's stature on the world stage in just a few words? For once, I was almost stumped for an opening line.

However, I did my 20-minute spot, which went very well, then turned to the assembled guests and said: "Ladies and gentlemen, the guest speaker today needs no introduction from me on this stage or any other stage in the world. Suffice it is to say that they are currently making his life story into a movie in Hollywood and they're trying to get Moses to play his part."

The audience fell about.

"Ladies and gentlemen," I said. "Charlton Heston."

The man was a great and entertaining speaker and the audience hung on to his every word.

After the Middle East and Far East tours, back home there had been a shift in the entertainment scene; the clubs weren't packing them in like they used to and for a comic like me new territory and new sources of income needed to be explored.

The heyday of the club era, when the local club was the focal point of the community, was well and truly over. These were the clubs where some of the biggest names in show-business started their careers; clubs where punters had to get there at about 6.30pm to ensure they got a seat in the concert room. Now the clubs were dying a death, most struggling to survive with a dwindling membership, a hardcore of few regular customers and a lack of demand for star turns. Even the bingo – a regular source of income for clubs – was being taken over by the big firms, opening bingo clubs here there and everywhere. Those who ventured out at a weekend preferred pub crawls to sitting in smoke-filled concert rooms and the growth in home entertainment, videos, DVDs, combined with all the other changes on the entertainment scene, saw many big, once-profitable clubs, close down or put their owners on the brink of bankruptcy.

It really was the end of an era.

*　*　*　*　*　*　*

The big man Adrian Marshall and Sunderland football coach Kevin Ball cringed when I pulled back my pyjama top and showed them the scar that ran from one side of my body to the other. The pair were just two of the scores of visitors to my home in Farringdon after I had left hospital and was confined to my bed to recuperate. Inevitably, with the team doing so badly, talk got round to football, the distinct possibility of relegation from the Premiership, and what had contributed to the recent poor run of results. It was all very sad.

"We've got to give the lads all the support we can," I said, "especially at a time when they're doing so badly."

"Things are looking bleak," said Adrian.

"Bleak?" I asked. "If they get any worse they'll fall off the bottom of the coupon."

"Do you know," I said. "There was something on the news the other night about this bloke in the sea about to be attacked by a great white shark. The shark approached and the bloke just stuck his forearm out, the shark took one look, then scarpered. The shark came back for another go, and the bloke again just stuck his forearm out and the shark retreated."

"Why did it do that, then?" Adrian asked.

"Because the fella had a tattoo on his arm."

"And what did the tattoo say?" Asked Adrian.

" 'Sunderland for the Premiership title' … and there's no fucker will swallow that."

Chapter Eighteen

CLOSE ENCOUNTERS

Comedian Tom O'Connor was not getting a lot of laughs on stage at Joe Foster's club, Close Encounters of the Third Kind, on Sunderland's Barbary Coast, and the anticipated sell-out crowd had failed to materialise; there was about 100 people in the audience. Joe was standing at the bar, drinking pint after pint, and moaning.

"I'm not fucking paying him full whack," said Joe.

"You'll have to pay him," I said. "It's not Tom's fault the club isn't packed."

At the end of Tom's session, he came off stage and I walked with him over to the bar to see Joe Foster.

"Joe," I said. "This is Tom O'Connor, who you've already met, and this is his road manager, a former European heavyweight champion."

"Great show, Tom," said Joe. "I'll get you your cash."

I first met Joe Foster, who became a good friend, in the La Strada nightclub in Sunderland in about 1975 when I was flitting in and out of the country from Africa. At the time I was quite a big celebrity and, with the stunning Diane on my arm, whenever we made an entrance into a club or pub it was always an entrance, heads would turn and people would flock towards us.

Joe had taken over a pub called The Welcome Tavern in the East End and whenever I was home from my travels I would pop in to see him and have a Bacardi and Coke, chew the fat and discuss business. Joe had a good brain on him, was something of an entrepreneur, and had a lot of contacts in the business. It was the start of a business partnership that has lasted well over 25 years.

He opened a nightclub in Sunderland called Fosters and one of the first shows we staged there was a bit of a stag do for motor traders. It was the usual type of stag night with a pie and peas supper, a couple of strippers, myself the comedian, and the punters downing copious amounts of alcohol. It could have been a good night, if the strippers Joe had booked had been a little more attractive than the doormen and if the other two strippers had bothered to turn up at all.

We were in for a difficult night.

"You can't go on too early," said Joe. "I'll not sell any beer."

We dragged the first part of the night out a little bit, then the strippers went on, did their business, and came off, and everything seemed to be going well. But there was the little problem of not having anything else by way of entertainment for the lads who, by this time, had downed so much beer they were becoming restless and agitated.

We decided, foolishly, to put the strippers on again. That's when all hell broke loose. First there were a few audible complaints, a lot of abuse hurled at the dancers, and then the sparks ignited for a near riot.

I took to the stage, took control, and after only five minutes I had the lads eating out of my hands.

Although a lot of the clubs were closing down at this time, the Sunderland Empire, as ever, was doing good business and a few of the stars I met there, such as Charlie Williams, Bobby Ball and Windsor Davies, joined me for a drink in Fosters club after the shows. Often I could persuade them to do a ten-minute slot at the club and I would get up myself to entertain the crowd.

Joe Foster later took over a big club, The Boilermakers' Club, at Monkwearmouth, refurbished it, re-named it Close Encounters and asked me to help him attract some big name acts to the club. Among the stars we booked were Lena Zavaroni and The Drifters. We arranged a big cabaret night and Joe started advertising, before he'd been granted a licence and the inevitable happened. During an inspection someone discovered a very minor fault in the emergency back-up lighting system and we had to cancel the acts.

The north of England, once the mecca for club-land entertainment, was going through a rough time, what with the closure of the shipyards and the coal mines and little cash floating about for people to spend in the clubs.

But thousands of people were soon to flock to an entertainment centre which attracted some of the best cabaret stars in the world. The centre – the McEwan's Centre in Houghton-le-Spring – looked like nothing more than an aircraft hangar and the thought of this being turned into the biggest entertainment complex in the north of England at first appeared laughable.

Joe Foster and I were approached by local businessman and self-made millionaire Matt Roseberry who was losing cash hand over fist keeping the McEwan's Centre open as an indoor cricket centre for up-and-coming young cricketers. Matt also had a vision of bringing first-class cricket to County Durham and the McEwan's Centre was very much at the centre of that vision.

Matt, like me, was very much a Sunderland lad, born in Southwick and growing up in Pennywell and Thorney Close, he had always been true to his roots. His was a life started from humble beginnings and he had worked hard to build up what was becoming a multi-million pound construction and pub and hotel empire.

He had started work at 15 as an apprentice bricklayer at Wearmouth Colliery but soon moved into building stone fireplaces, then building houses, then owning pubs and hotels. But his two biggest passions in life were Sunderland Football Club and cricket. His son Michael became a full-time professional with Middlesex and his second son Andrew signed for Leicester.

The McEwan's Centre, built by Matt's firm Roseberry Construction, was mirrored on Lord's Indoor Cricket School and had all the best facilities young cricketers could be offered. The turf was the best on the market and youngsters could practise on six different lanes. The talented young batsmen and bowlers using the nets at McEwan's would become the first class cricketers for County Durham, Matt would enthuse.

But running the centre was proving a drain on finances. The rates for the building alone were £20,000 a year, the electricity bill was about £15,000 a year and the annual insurance bill was about £10,000. If the centre was being used to its full capacity, with 25 cricketers using the nets at £1 per hour each, that was only bringing in £25 per hour. Matt Roseberry knew that if the centre was to survive, along with his dream of first class cricket for County Durham, he would have to diversify. Enter Joe Foster, with a background in pub and club management, and enter Bobby Knoxall, with the contacts and the know-how within the entertainment business that Matt Roseberry would need if his efforts to bank-roll the cricket centre were to succeed.

It was the start of a successful business venture that would last 11 years and would see some of the world's top entertainers perform on Wearside.

*　*　*　*　*　*　*

My mate Bill Tipling rolled up his trouser leg to show me the scar from his recent operation to have a knee replaced.

"I don't want to see your fucking scar," I said. "I've had enough of scars to last me a lifetime."

Our house was turning into a refuge for the recently hospitalised elderly. Here was Bill, with a new knee, Jackie Longstaff was in the living room talking about his recent operation and the benefits to his diet of drinking red wine, and here was I flat out on my back recuperating after a major operation.

Bill was having to use a walking stick, Jackie was using a walking stick, and I could barely walk. And the talk would often turn to our ailments, or our bowels. It always seemed strange to me that people who were getting on in years often talked about their bowel movements. They seemed preoccupied with the subject, and here we were talking about the same. We were all getting on in years, so I suppose chatting about the subject was inevitable really, however distasteful it may seem to others.

"Bill," I said. "Did you hear on the news the other day about the bloke wanted by Scotland yard who wanted to lay low for a few weeks?"

"No," said Bill.

"Yes," I said. "He's been hiding out in the Ivy Leaf Club. No bugger will think of looking for him there."

Bill, a regular at the Ivy Leaf Club in Hendon, saw the funny side. He, like me, had seen the death of the workingmen's clubs.

Bill had been campaigning for a few months to try to get me an honour for all the charity work I had done over the last 50 or so years. It was a kind gesture and Bill had been contacting as many top local councillors, MPs and other local big wigs as possible to try and gain their support. He had met with some success.

It was Bill who had instigated the campaign, I had nothing to do with it, but I was flattered that he had gone to such lengths to try and get me on to the honours list. Bobby Knoxall, MBE, had a nice ring to it, as did even Bobby Knoxall OBE or CBE. Sir Robert of Loxley was my favourite title, but that, of course, was a joke I shared with people when they started name-dropping.

Since my operation and with myself out of hospital but housebound I had a great deal of time on my hands to think and plan for the future. When fit again, I wanted to write my life story and produce a video. Many other comedians had produced videos and it was something I had given some thought to, but never got round to actually doing something about it.

I wanted to do so much. I wanted to raise a lot more money for charity, after reading about the plight of others in the local newspaper.

I had big plans to tour again, to travel abroad; to do what I did best, making people laugh.

It seemed I had a hell of a lot to do, but it appeared I had so little time left in which to do it.

Chapter Nineteen

ELVIS AT ROKER

His raven-black hair was slicked back with just a short, wispy, quiff resting on his forehead. His black leather trousers fitted where they touched and his long, flowing, black coat almost touched his shins. James Rampel, who looked uncannily like The King in his youth, looked the business and as we walked towards Roker Park for the big match hundreds of pairs of eyes rested on him, most in admiration, some in envy.

Then, just as the dark clouds had threatened, the heavens opened and down poured the rain. The dye in his hair ran down his heavily made-up face and the illusion was shattered. The King had gone and in his place was the young pretender.

"Is he with you?" I asked Matt Roseberry.

"He's fucking not with me," said Matt, as he headed off in front.

"Well, he's fucking not with me," I said, as I made a detour through Roker, heading for the ground.

We could have been out of Matt's car and in the ground within a couple of minutes, if someone hadn't nicked his parking space. But they had, and Matt had to park a few minutes walk away from Roker Park, and join the throng on its way to the turnstiles, with myself and our Elvis lookalike.

James Rampel was a big hit in the United States, wowing the crowds with his Elvis impersonations. Not only did he look exactly like The King, he moved and sang like him, too.

Matt Roseberry, myself and Joe Foster had flown to Las Vegas on a talent-spotting tour when we saw James playing at the Desert Inn, alongside some other mirror images of the big stars, such as an Elton John lookalike. Matt met James for lunch in Caesar's Palace the following day and persuaded him to sign a six-month contract to come over to England to perform, with yours truly, at the McEwan's Centre and at some of the big clubs in the North East where cabaret was still on the menu.

James was an instant hit, making a dramatic entrance into the McEwan's Centre, looking every inch like the young Elvis Presley, and matching his visual performance with near perfect renditions of some of Elvis's greatest hits.

The only problem was, he would sing only three or four songs, so he was only ever on stage no more than 20 minutes. There was no way he could tour other cabaret clubs in the north of England with an act so short.

The audiences at the McEwan's Centre loved him but James was only of the big stars whose services we managed to secure, which made McEwan's the entertainment centre of the North. The stunning Tina Turner look and sound-a-like Suzette Dorsey was one of the acts we booked and there were many other sound-alikes and tribute bands.

But the icing on the cake were the big original artistes we managed to sign up; international Grammy-award winning superstar Gloria Gaynor, The Supremes, led by Mary Wilson, The Drifters, Jimmy Cricket, Les Dennis, Showaddywaddy, Duncan Norvelle, Marty Wilde, Tony Christie and his band, six members of the soul band The Commitments, The Searchers, The Stylistics, The Crystals and many more.

Not since the days of the La Strada and Wetherells in Sunderland had there been so much cabaret talent in one place on offer to audiences in the North East. And with such talent topping the bill, it was clear from day one that the McEwan's Centre was going to be a soarway success.

It had all got off to something of a shaky start when Matt Roseberry contacted me and outlined his plans for the centre. He knew I had the contacts to attract the right acts, Joe Foster had the experience of managing big pubs and clubs, and what Matt could offer was something very much needed, an open cheque book.

We travelled to London to meet an agent at London Management – where I bumped into my old boss Peter Elliott – but it was clear the man we were dealing with regarded us as ten-bob, know-nothing northerners out of their depth. It didn't help our credibility when Matt Roseberry told the man he would like to book Shirley Bassey.

However, when it became known that Matt Roseberry was a multi-millionaire who meant business, we proceeded to do business. As ever, money was doing the talking.

After our successful afternoon negotiations we decided to have a night in the west end and a nice meal and ended back at our hotel a little more than slightly intoxicated. Matt ordered a round of drinks as a nightcap … then all hell broke loose.

Matt was not too happy that the drinks' bill was far higher than expected, he was being charged for doubles when he only ordered singles.

"I'm fucking not paying for this," he said, and left the drinks on the bar.

Then he explained to the Chinese barman that he had not ordered doubles, but singles, and singles is all he would pay for.

"You can't have singles," the barman said, "this is a doubles bar."

Matt was bloody furious and demanded to see the manager. The assistant manager, who happened to be on duty, arrived and tried to defuse what had become quite a volatile situation. Here we were, a comedian, two businessmen and a lawyer who was also in our company, arguing the toss with two Chinamen and the hotel was in uproar. This situation was meant for television comedy sketches, not for weary travellers who had spent a hard day in negotiations and just wanted a nightcap without any fuss.

Matt was adamant. The barman and the assistant manager were also adamant and a heated argument almost developed into fisticuffs.

Hotel security was called for, and the police, and within minutes we were on the Tottenham Court Road, heavily laden with our suitcases, at three in the morning, with not a taxi in sight, and it was pissing it down with rain.

"I told them, didn't I?" Said Matt.

"You certainly did that, Matt," I said. "You certainly did that."

There were several more trips to London to arrange acts for the McEwan's Centre and, often, Matt would call into see his son Michael who by then was playing cricket for Middlesex.

The runaway success of the McEwan's Centre as the mecca for entertainment in the North for 11 years, in the run up to each Christmas, wasn't just a stroke of luck for Matt Roseberry, who was looking to bankroll his efforts to keep the centre up and running for young cricketers and head for his ultimate dream, first class cricket for County Durham. It was a success because of Matt's cash and business acumen, my contacts within the entertainment business, and the managerial know-how of Joe Foster and Mike Weston.

My only problem with the centre was one of communication. Whenever I called to speak to Matt Roseberry I would be told he was out, and if I tried to speak to Mike Weston, I would be told he was tied up. It seemed Matt would tie up Mike whenever he left the building.

There were other problems associated with the centre, such as acts not turning up on time, or not at all, or ticket sales not going as well as forecast, and, often, I would be called upon to help out when things were going pear-shaped.

One night comedian Jimmy Cricket was scheduled to perform and 700 people were waiting to hear his show, but Jimmy was lost in fog on his way up north. A few frantic telephone calls later and I found myself in front of the 700-strong crowd, giving it my best shot. I tore the balls off them, metaphorically speaking, putting on a performance that had them laughing for almost an hour, and by the time Jimmy turned up, and took to the stage, I had well and truly stolen his thunder. I was a hard act to follow at the best of times, as many comedians knew to their cost, and poor Jimmy must have wished he had stayed in the fog. Jimmy's fee for the night was several hundred pounds, which he was paid, and Mike Weston gave me a tenner. I framed it.

Before his rise to fame on television Les Dennis was booked to appear at the McEwan's Centre but ticket sales were not going well and Matt Roseberry rang Les's agent and asked him to cancel, offering him £1,500 for his trouble anyway, but the agent wouldn't have it. He insisted that Les, as per his contract, appeared at the centre. Matt put someone else in and asked Les to appear at another of his venues, The Chilton Country Pub and Hotel in Fence Houses, near Sunderland, and Les spent the night signing autographs. The future Family Fortunes host wasn't happy. He said he could have done with a night off anyway and would have accepted a mere £500 to cancel his appearance. His agent, of course, would have lost his percentage cut if that had happened.

With the demise of the workingmen's clubs, another avenue for entertainers, particularly comedians, was the sportsmen's dinners – evenings of entertainment where the guest speaker, someone who had made it big in the sporting world, would recount interesting tales from their past and amuse the audience with many anecdotes. One of the first such speakers booked at the McEwan's Centre was George Best, the twinkle-toed Irishman who dazzled football fans with his amazing skills on the pitch and amazed pub landlords off the pitch with his amazing ability to drink copious amounts of alcohol. He turned up for the show absolutely rat-arsed and yours truly was called upon again to save the day. George just sat in the audience listening to my jokes, and appeared to enjoy himself.

Matt Roseberry mainly used the Chilton County Pub and Hotel as the venue for sportsmen's dinners, and I was often the "top class" comedian fronting the shows. Among the speakers I introduced was Bobby Robson, at the time the England team manager and later Sir Bobby Robson, manager of Newcastle United, cricketing legend Ian Botham, Tommy Docherty, the former manager of Manchester United and Malcolm MacDonald, ex England and Newcastle United football star.

My association with footballers, and appearing on the bill when they were guest speakers, went way back. I had been associated with Sunderland Football Club since the early 1960s and counted Charlie Hurley, one of the greatest footballers ever to have played for my home side, among my friends. Charlie was also a talented after-dinner speaker.

The McEwan's Centre staged one of the biggest sportsmen's dinners ever held in the North East when Gary Bennett retired from Sunderland AFC, and I was there to entertain the crowds.

With the demise of the workingmen's clubs it seemed obvious to me that these sportsmen's dinners – nights of interesting conversation and comedy – were one avenue for making a crust. I threw myself into them.

And, as well as the after-dinner chats about football, I teamed up with a well-known Sunderland boxing promoter, Tommy Conroy, to help him with the sporting club he had set up. Tommy attracted some very big hitters to the North East and I was very impressed, as he had never made it big in the ring himself. I often joked – and Tommy always accepted the joke as it was intended – that he was the only boxer I knew who had a cauliflower arse.

But, joking aside, Tommy Conroy had a good track record as an amateur boxer, taking to the ring in 89 or so fights, and, more importantly, Tommy spotted and nurtured boxing talent in the North East like few others involved in the game did. He was, and still is, truly committed to the game. He has always been as passionate about boxing as Matt Roseberry was passionate about cricket.

Tommy Conroy is the only person I have ever known who has a boxing ring and a gym in his own house. Most people would settle for a three-piece suite and a television. Tommy and I reached an agreement that I would support him, and his sporting club, as long as I could and, in turn, when he produced a big-hitting champion, I would still be on board.

Ours was a partnership forged out of hard work and hope. Tommy only ever broke even staging his sporting club dinners, which included a few rounds of boxing, but he, and I, lived in hope that one day he would find a champion.

* * * * * * *

I was starting to eat a little better, building up my strength, and since leaving hospital I must have put on about three stone. The signs were positive and I was hopeful that I soon might be able to get back on stage.

There was a boxing show coming up, and a charity function, and Joe Foster was planning a bit of a comeback night for me at the River Wear Social Club in Hendon. All that depended on me getting back on my feet.

One of the most touching gestures by my many friends during my recuperation was a tribute to Bobby Knoxall night held in Sunderland which raised £6,000 for myself and my family. The cash was a Godsend because I obviously couldn't work, did not have a brass farthing to my name, and bills had to be paid.

It wasn't the first time friends had rallied to help me out in a time of

210

need. After my heart attack in the Middle East, when Judith Durham was so good to me, I was laid up on the sidelines for several months. I couldn't pay myself sick pay. Joe Foster and my then agent Bob Gladwin pulled out all the stops to hold a tribute night and many of the show-business friends I had worked with in the past gave their services free of charge, among them Mike Reid and ventriloquist Roger de Courcey. The night was held in the McEwan's Centre and was a great success, raising several thousands of pounds to tide me and my family over until I got myself fit again.

That heart attack came only five months after a previous seizure and I blamed myself, really. I had not given myself enough time to recuperate before taking to the stage again. That was my problem. I had always been very fit and active, and couldn't abide sitting around doing nothing. From my days jumping from the mantelpiece in Sunderland's Norfolk Hotel and doing the splits, right up to the present day, I had always been a livewire.

Joe Foster, when publicising the tribute night, stressed how much I had raised for charity over the years and how this was an opportunity for people to give something back to a veteran North East comedian who had given so much to his home town. He was right, I had raised hundreds of thousands of pounds for charity since I started my career almost 50 years earlier, but I didn't expect to get anything back from it. I did charity work because I wanted to.

As I sat in my favourite armchair, looking back on things that had gone, another veteran entertainer now suffering ill health, Jackie Longstaff came into the room. Jackie had been through a number of operations and, like me, was having to take things easy.

He had just returned from the shops, with two stottie cake sandwiches. My appetite was such I could have eaten a scabby horse.

Jackie offered me both sandwiches and I, naturally, took the biggest and started tucking in.

"You're a great friend, you are," said Jackie.

"How's that like?" I asked.

"You took the biggest sandwich."

"Well, which one would you have taken?" I asked.

"I would have taken the smaller one," said Jackie, "and left the big one for you."

"Well, that's the one you've got," I said.

Jackie had been a regular visitor to my home for many years and it was nice to see him popping in as often as he could during my convalescence. We had such a history together, stretching back more than 50 years, we could spark off each other, rekindle memories that had lain dormant for so long, and it was this type of banter that kept my spirits up.

Being stuck in the house and waiting, just waiting, to recover could be so soul destroying. It was nice to have people around me who cared because with such people around me I knew I was not fighting my battle for fitness alone.

Chapter Twenty

A FEW ROUNDS

World heavyweight boxer Ernie Shavers was a formidable character, towering above everyone else at the top table at one of Tommy Conroy's sporting club dinners and the audience was spell-bound as he recounted some of the stories from his glittering career.

"I got two hundred thousand dollars when I fought Mohammed Ali," he said. "And I got half a million when I fought Larry Holmes."

After his speech I grabbed the microphone and said: "That's very impressive. I fought Butchy Craig and Benny the Brick, and I got fuck all."

Ernie, a real nice guy, was a great speaker. He recounted how he knocked Mohammed Ali on to the canvas and for seven seconds, just seven seconds, he was the World Heavyweight Champion of the world.

Another of his stories centred on a conversation he had with his wife about the fortune he had made in the ring. He said he asked her if he did not have such a fortune, and was not so famous, would she still love him. His woman said of course she would still love him. She'd miss him, but she would still love him.

I had first met Ernie Shavers several years earlier in London, when I worked for London Management, when we did a dinner one night for Henry Cooper, who was then British champion, in the Bloomsbury Hotel.

He was one of many boxers I met during my career who would later grace the top table at one of Tommy Conroy's boxing dinners in Sunderland. Another was John Conteh, whom I met in Kirby when Jackie Longstaff and I were touring the clubs in Liverpool. John was making a big name for himself then in the amateur boxing world and I knew he would make it big in the professional game.

Tommy Conroy was able to attract many high-profile guest speakers to his dinners, held initially at the Crowtree Leisure Centre in Sunderland then later the Swallow Hotel, later to become the Marriott Hotel. Many of the speakers were well-known boxers, promoters or managers, among them Brendan Ingle and John Conteh, but some were footballers, such as Ali McCoist and he was also able to attract big names in snooker, such as Barry Hearn, who did a number of shows, and Steve Davis.

I made a deal with Tommy that I would host the shows for him and either provide a comedian or do the comedy myself and, though Tommy always ever only broke even on the nights, they were a great success. There was some terrific bouts of boxing, too, and I was able to watch many young hopefuls coming through the ranks.

The East End of Sunderland had produced some of the best fighters in the North East in the ring, and some of the hardest men who fought outside of the ring and fighting, like football, had always interested me.

From the age of 17 I had associated with hard cases and witnessed many bare-knuckle, toe-to-toe fights in the streets and back lanes of the East End or on the Town Moor. The hard cases I had met in Sunderland, Newcastle and elsewhere, were all people I came to respect and, in some ways, admired. I was never among the higher ranks of the hard cases myself, but I could handle myself and, as Sunderland's first kick-boxing street-fighter, I earned myself something of a reputation as a man not to be messed with and my older brother Jonty could look after himself, too.

Sunderland's most famous boxer, Cast Iron Casey, played dominoes in The Three Crowns, where I collected glasses as a boy, and I talked to him quite a lot. He never smoked but always accepted cigarettes, probably to take home to his wife.

At weekends there was always street fights in the town, someone wanting to have a go, reputations to be challenged but, often, some of the men would just fight for fun whilst bets were placed amongst those looking on.

I had a few fights myself as a boy, there was three boxing clubs in Sunderland when I was a teenager, but never showed any real promise. I didn't really have the enthusiasm or the commitment to take boxing up even in the amateur game. To succeed in the ring takes dedication and bloody hard work and I have a lot of admiration for fighters.

Tommy Conroy, whose sport was football in his teens, had entered boxing at the relatively late age of 25, initially training with Tommy Comiskey. Tommy and Charlie Graham had got a boxing gym going down at the old East End Boys' Orphanage and Tommy later started training kids from the streets. He later teamed up with Frankie Deans, from South Shields, started the coaching of Sunderland Amateur Boxing Club and went into the professional game in about 1981, taking such boxers under his wing as John Davidson, who went on to box for British, European and World titles.

Tommy had 16 fighters at one time training at the gym he had attached to his house.

The North East Sporting Executive Club was set up in about 1995 and Tommy approached me to ask me to look after the top table at the club's dinners and book comedians. As I had always been interested in sport, both football and boxing, I was delighted to be able to help out. They were, and still are, great nights providing entertainment for about 200 people, which includes a hardcore of about 150 supporters of the sport who turn up at virtually every do.

Tommy, whose has done more to promote boxing in Sunderland than any other, is still waiting for his first champion, but one lad coming through the ranks now, Ryan Kerr, certainly has the potential to be a number one contender at his weight.

The North East Sporting Club dinners have kept me in the limelight, if not in wages, and I have been privileged to have met some of the country's top sporting stars in the world of football, boxing, snooker and those who promote sports.

But there were two other fighters that I met away from Tommy Conroy's sporting dinners whom I would never have encountered had I not made a career for myself in show-business and had never travelled the world.

One was Mohammed Ali and the other that legendary American boxer, Rocky Marciano.

Ali travelled to the North East to officially open a mosque in South Shields and later went on to attend a boxing dinner. My agent then was Hughie Turner, from Bedlington, Northumberland, and he joined me at the dinner where, among the top cabaret stars, were Jimmy Tarbuck and Kenny Lynch.

Ali was an enigma. He had the kind of presence and charisma that could overshadow anyone.

As for Marciano, to meet one of the greatest power punchers in boxing history, the only undefeated champion in any weight class, with 43 knock-outs in 49 fights and a perfect record of all wins, no losses and no draws, the Heavyweight Champion of the World from 1952 to his retirement in 1956, was probably the most memorable moment of my career. When I met Rocky Marciano I was dumbstruck.

It happened in Durban, South Africa, when Rocky, who wasn't that tall but compact and thick set, was the guest speaker at The Jewish Club, which attracted some of the biggest celebrities in the world for their annual dinners.

I was working for Peter Hubbard at the time and was breaking a few records myself, packing the crowds in at the Beach Hotel in Durban. An American comic, booked for the show with Rocky, had fallen ill and Peter Hubbard called me to ask if I could do the club, telling me he would find another comic to run the Crazy Horse for the few hours I was away. Peter didn't tell me who the guest speaker was at The Jewish Club and, to be honest, I never asked. Perhaps he wanted to surprise me.

The first thing that struck me about the club was the size of the place and the opulence of the furnishings and fittings. At the club entrance, just in the foyer, stood a huge board with the names of all the big stars who had appeared there in gold writing, such as Bob Hope and Danny Kaye. Near the board was a bill advertising that day's show and on it was the names Rocky Marciano and Bobby Knoxall. As I stood in the foyer, staring at the bill, I knew then that I had arrived.

When I met the man, the hairs on the back of my neck literally stood up. I had never been in such illustrious company. The man was a living legend and one of my all-time sporting heroes and I was standing next to him in a plush club thousands of miles away from home and a million miles away from anything else I had ever encountered.

Rocky was a gentleman, immediately putting me at ease, and gave one of the best after-dinner speeches I have ever heard. Afterwards we just sat and talked, for a couple of hours. He told me a little about his life, his upbringing and his fights, and I was utterly enthralled.

It was an encounter that would stay with me for the rest of my life and one that, I knew, would never be topped. Meeting such a world-famous star whose achievements have gone down in history, was a chance in a million.

I was thankful that the American comic had fallen ill, for it was his illness that had given me the opportunity. I was thankful, too, to my boss and great friend Peter Hubbard who signed me up for the job of a lifetime.

✻　✻　✻　✻　✻　✻　✻

I'd had a tip-off, from those supposedly in the know, for the 2.30pm at Kempton and as I watched the race on television, I cursed the fact that I had decided against a flutter. I'd decided against a bet because my gambling days were over. I just didn't get the adrenaline rush anymore and I had far better things to do with the little money I had.

Jackie Longstaff still liked a flutter, almost every day, and when his race was on the television his eyes were glued to the set and he did not take kindly to interruptions.

"Go on, my beauty," he said. "Go on, lass".

"She's heading for the knacker's yard, not the finishing post," I said.

"Shut up," said Jackie. "Fucking shut up."

Jackie had his walking stick by his side and was whacking himself on the leg, as if he was the jockey, getting himself all excited.

"Go on, lass," he said. "Go on!"

His expression of delight at an anticipated windfall quickly turned to one of despair when the old nag hobbled across the line in third place.

"I fucking told you you were wasting your money," I said.

"Wasting MY money? Wasting MY fucking money?" Said Jack, his face red and his eyes almost bulging out of their sockets.

"Why. You've got some fucking nerve, you have," he said. "That coming from a man who must have wasted two fucking million in his time."

I thought about the figure Jackie had plucked from the air for a moment and immediately concluded that he was exaggerating. But was he? I thought about it a little more, about the thousands I had gambled over the years, hundreds every week. It all added up and Jackie's figure was probably a conservative estimate.

"You know something, son," I said. "You're probably fucking right. I must have spent two million pounds on gambling, cigarettes, booze and women."

"Aye, aye, your right," said Jackie. "And you must have fucking wasted the rest."

It was a joke we shared regularly.

I had spent a fortune over the years on gambling, mainly horse racing, but had only seen the light a couple of years ago that it is only the bookie that ever wins. You can win once, but the cash soon finds its way back to the bookie's pockets.

In Jersey I had once won £14,000 on the horses – a huge sum in those days – and bought our two sons a present each, Diane a fantastic engagement ring and treated myself to a nice Rolex watch. Then I met up with a few pals in England and drove to Ascot in my Starliner car and blew a cool £3,000 on the horses. I came away absolutely skint and didn't even have enough petrol in my motor – which guzzled a gallon of petrol for every ten miles – and had to give the petrol pump attendant my Rolex watch in exchange for a tank-full of petrol which I would later redeem when I raised the cash to pay for the fuel. I was Jack the Lad, an award-winning comedian in Jersey, earning several hundreds of pounds every week.

My gambling days had started years earlier in the Ro Ko-Ko Club in Sunderland where I would play poker until the early hours of the morning with the likes of Ronnie Prenelle and other card-sharps, lose a couple of hundred quid, come away and think nothing of it. Money ran through my hands like water, but I knew I could always earn more cash by doing a club here or there. Often my gambling forced me into the position where I had to work, rather than wanted to work, and even though I enjoyed the work, in circumstances like that it could become something of a chore.

I had always done what I wanted to do, not what others told me, even if their advice was well-intentioned. A rebel, a hell-raiser, a hard-case, sometimes the hero, and sometimes the fool. My life has been one long roller-coaster ride with extreme highs and extreme lows; more ups and downs than the proverbial tart's knickers. And I wouldn't change a thing.

"Mr Knoxall," said Jackie.

"What?" I asked.

"Will you be partaking of high tea?"

"High tea," I said. "High tea. Have you already had luncheon?"

"I've had a sandwich," said Jackie.

"Diane," I shouted through to the kitchen.

"Can you put the kettle on please, love"

Jackie and I turned our attention to the next race and he picked up his walking stick.

"Mind you don't get too excited," I said. "You'll end up with bruises on your thighs."

Chapter Twenty One

OFF THE PITCH

The top VIPs in Eire were in the audience, among them the sporting elite, Finbar Furey from that great Irish band The Fureys, a few members of the Irish parliament; almost all of them distinguished members of the southern Irish hoy poloy and all gathered for the worthwhile cause of raising cash to send an Irish team off to compete in the Paralympics.

One of the organisers of the high-profile event was a man who had become a good friend of mine, the big man Niall Quinn, former Irish international football star, doing wonders for Sunderland at the Stadium of Light, and a man whose charitable nature knew no bounds, as witnessed by him donating ALL, yes ALL, the proceeds from his testimonial match at Sunderland towards charity.

But tonight big Niall was worried. It wasn't that the event wasn't going well; it was actually going swimmingly. It wasn't that huge amounts of cash were not being raised, the event was raising thousands. No, what worried big Niall was the fact that Bobby Knoxall was about to stand up and crack a few gags in front of an almost all-Irish audience.

"No racist gags. And definitely no Irish gags," Niall whispered in my ear. "And please, please, please, keep it clean."

Niall had his heart in his mouth when I stood up with the microphone in my hand. I really felt for the kid. But I knew how to handle an audience, and I knew how far I could go.

"Good evening, ladies and gentlemen," I said, in my most focused of deliveries. "My name is Bobby Knoxall."

Niall gave me a worried glance. I ignored him.

"I love the Irish. Do you know, my grandfather was Irish," I said. "He came over to England during the potato famine. Except it wasn't a famine, was it? You lot just forgot where you planted them."

Some of the audience burst into laughter, some fell into stunned silence, others lifted their eyes to the heavens disapprovingly and Niall buried his head in his hands.

"I was baptised a Roman Catholic, you know," I said. "But I don't go to church now. Now I'm more of a roaming catholic."

"Good evening Father," I said to everyone's astonishment. "I see Father Nicholas has graced us with his presence this evening. Very nice to see you father.

"Now, just the other week, Father Nicholas, a keen cyclist, walked by my house and I asked him where his bike was. He told me it had been stolen.

" 'Really', I said. 'That's awful'. I told the Father that all he needed to do was at next Sunday's mass read out the Ten Commandments and when he came to Thou Shalt Not Steal, a quick look around the congregation would reveal the identity of the thief, as guilt would be written all over their face.

"I saw Father Nicholas a week later, riding his bicycle. I said to him. 'Oh, Father, I see you have your bike back. Did you do as I had suggested?' The priest said he had and it worked wonders. Then did you catch the thief? I asked. Father Nicholas replied that he hadn't. He read through the Ten Commandments, came to Thou Shalt Not Commit Adultery, then remembered where he had left his bike."

The audience roared with laughter, Niall Quinn sank his head further into his hands, but Bobby Knoxall then knew he had connected with the audience, and I was flying.

In the corner of my eye I spotted a rather large woman, neatly dressed, all prim and proper, sitting next to her husband, a thin and small ineffectual guy who I could see from just looking at was under the almighty thumb.

My antennae honed in.

"You know, ladies and gentleman, I'm something of a clairvoyant," I said. "I can read the cards, tea leaves and all that. And I can tell a person's star sign just by looking at them. Come on, test me out, raise your hands."

The prim woman raised her hand.

"You're Leo, aren't you," I said.

"No," said the woman. "I'm Pisces."

"I should have known, madam," I said. "Pisces – big mouthed bastard who always speaks out first."

The night was going great guns, even though I had toned down my act, and when my 30-minute or so spot came to an end, I said: "Well, thank you ladies and gentlemen, I'll see you all next Christmas because I've just heard the concert secretary say, 'it'll be a bloody cold night before we book him again'."

As I made my way to the bar, the prim woman was straight on to her feet and heading towards me like an Exocet missile.

"I think you were funny, but you were far too arrogant," she said. "And I don't think you should come over here and belittle the Irish."

"I do apologise madam, if I offended you," I said. "But I've been doing this act for years and I'm very successful."

"You had no right taking the mick out of the Irish," she said.

"I am sorry," I said, feigning pity. "I really haven't been the same since I lost my wife."

The prim woman was taken aback. "Oh. I am sorry. I didn't realise..." she said.

"It was the best game of cards I've had for a long time," I said.

The woman, insulted, turned and stormed off. But her manner did not upset me, or put a damper on the rest of the trip.

Several of the Sunderland footballers had joined the group travelling to Eire with Niall Quinn and my great friend, and equally fanatical Sunderland supporter, Adrian Marshall, was also with us.

Adrian's links with the football team, and many of its current and former players, went back years, but not as far back as my own association with the club.

Adrian, a larger-than-life character, was born in Seaham but spent most of his life growing up in Sunderland, worked for a spell as an assistant manager at the town's Crowtree Leisure Centre, where I first met him, and took over a pub called The Phoenix in Seaham during the turbulent Miners' Strike of 1984. It was a difficult time for anyone starting a business in an area where working down the pits was a town's main source of income, but Adrian made a success of the pub and turned one of the bars in it into a shrine to Sunderland AFC.

Later, Adrian took over The Alexandra pub in Grangetown, Sunderland, a popular bar with a huge function room, and made that a success, too, hosting many sportsmen's dinners and charity functions that raised lots of cash for local causes.

I had worked with football players for more than four decades since the 1960s, stars such as Charlie Hurley, George Best, Len Shackleton, Dennis Law, Tommy Docherty, Jack Charlton, Nobby Stiles, Billy Bremner, Bobby Robson, Malcolm MacDonald – all footballing legends who made a name for themselves on the after-dinner speaking circuit once their careers on the pitch had come to an end.

I was still friendly with some of Sunderland's famous 1973 FA Cup winning side, Jimmy Montgomery, Mickey Horswill and Bobby Kerr, for example, and I was still on first-name terms with many current members of the squad, and the new team manager Mick McCarthy. Club coach Kevin Ball, like big Niall Quinn, I could count as a personal friend.

My friendship with Niall really started when he and fellow players were out for a meal at a restaurant in Durham City with their wives and the night fell a little flat. They craved some entertainment, so Niall called me up and asked me to go over and crack a few gags. I did, and it was appreciated by everyone.

During our tour of Eire there was 16 of us on a coach travelling all over the place. Niall was taking part in a golf tournament, and we also spent a day at the races. I wasn't feeling too well, health-wise, and the lads had to basically carry me some of the way. It was the start of what was to become the worst period of ill health in my life.

Southern Ireland, for me, was absolutely amazing. The scenery was breathtaking, the people the friendliest I have ever met (second only to Sunderland folk), the towns and villages spotlessly clean and the church-es in each town veritable cathedrals, each with the most ornate architec-ture and a towering spire that symbolised what is, for the Irish, the most important building in the locality.

What I found really strange travelling around the country and look-ing out of the window in our coach, was the brightly and multi-coloured houses in some towns; one red, then one blue, then one yellow, then one green, perhaps reflecting their owners' individuality, the one area of Irish life where conformity was not required.

As we travelled through one town a giant Drive-Thru McDonald's restaurant shone like a beacon in the early evening, as obvious as shit on a barn door. It stuck out like a sore thumb, like a garish carbuncle in a row of quaint houses, the character of the town destroyed in one fell swoop.

"He's come a bloody long way since running that farm," I said, rousing everyone on the coach to look out of the windows.

"Who?" Asked Adrian Marshall.

"Old McDonald," I said.

Everyone laughed, but they could see how out-of-place the McDonalds looked in the small, rustic, old-fashioned town we travelled through.

Niall Quinn's fundraising drive to send athletes to the Paralympics during our tour of Eire was typical of the man; the Mighty Quinn was known to have a big heart. He joined Sunderland AFC in 1996 and became a great ambassador for the club, for the city, and for the professional game.

When Sunderland played the Republic of Ireland in Niall's testimonial match at the Stadium of Light in May 2002 people were astounded when he announced all of the proceeds from the game would be given over to charity. Such generosity from a top football player was unprecedented. Niall did it not to focus attention on himself – such a humble sportsman who would rather shun the limelight you're not likely to meet – he did it because he genuinely wanted to give something back through the game he loved to the charities he cared about. He had made a good living from football – he just wanted to give something back.

The £1million from his benefit game went to children's charities in Sunderland, in Dublin and in India. Sunderland Royal Hospital – formerly the General Hospital – was given £450,000 of the cash raised towards the building of a new children's outpatients' unit.

At a time when football is dominated by greed, with record transfer fees, record gate receipts and record ticket prices, Niall's amazing charitable gesture astounded everyone. But, knowing the man as I do, it didn't surprise me.

Recently Niall was given an Honorary MBE for his outstanding services to international football and his contributions to United Kingdom charities. It was an honour richly deserved.

I have always, personally, felt a great deal of pride to be associated with Sunderland Football Club and its players, and particularly to have the privilege of counting Niall Quinn among my friends.

* * * * * * *

The great love of my life, the brick, the pillar of strength when I was at my weakest moment, my beautiful wife Diane, had devoted her considerable energy, and care, to helping me through my convalescence. At the same time she was caring for three of our boys, Robert, Ryan and Brent. Our second eldest John was today to be married and it would be the first time the Knoxall family would be seen out together as a family for more than two years.

It was something of a double celebration, as Ryan, our second youngest, was celebrating his birthday, and the balloons and the bunting adorned our house as the celebrations got under way.

My great friend, and the man who had made such a huge impact on my show-business career, Ken Wayne, was travelling from his London home, with his social worker minder, to attend the wedding, staying at The Ramside Hall Hotel near Durham City.

I had ventured out of the house in recent months, to the occasional charity night, or after-dinner speech, a boxing do and the night at the club in Hendon.

But today was something different. I wouldn't be out of the house for an hour or two, I'd be out of the house all day, and it was the biggest test of endurance during my recuperation so far.

At the Ewesley Road Methodist Church in Sunderland, my son John looked the business in his wedding suit, as did our three other boys Robert, Ryan and Brent, and the bride, Maureen Evans, was resplendent.

In the aisles sat Tommy Conroy and his wife, Joe Foster and his wife, an extremely talented singer voted the best in North East club-land that year, Shaun Conley, and his partner, and many, many, more friends Diane and I had met over the years.

The service went like a dream and it was a proud day for the Knoxall family, particularly for our son John. After the wedding, it was down to The Alexandra pub in Grangetown for the reception, which many of our other friends attended.

I felt OK, I wasn't drinking, but after two hours or so in The Alexandra, I was suddenly overcome by the most overwhelming spell of dizziness I had ever known. Within two minutes, I was sitting outside the pub, in a chair which several people had carried me outside in, gasping for breath. It didn't last too long and soon I was back in the pub, having regained my composure, and my dizzy spell was forgotten.

Perhaps I had been on my feet too long that day, or perhaps the elation I felt at again meeting so many old friends had enveloped me to such an extent that I was overwhelmed.

Whatever it was, I knew it would be some time before I was back to my normal self, back to the kind of fitness where I could take to the stage and feel comfortable knowing that I could deliver.

It was hard to accept, but the fact was, I was still too weak.

Chapter Twenty Two

CHARITY BEGINS AT HOME

The man lying in a trolley hospital bed had just had treatment and was waiting for a porter to take him to his ward. As I sat waiting in the accident and emergency unit at Sunderland General Hospital, I got chatting to the man, who was from Ryhope, Sunderland, who told me he had been involved in a road accident. He had suffered broken bones, bruising and severe whiplash and when he was rushed to hospital in an ambulance he was having real difficulty breathing.

He told me he had had treatment a couple of days earlier when he was put on a new respiratory machine, a Barnet Mark III ventilator, which kind of acts as a "lung" helping the patient to breathe. He didn't recognise me.

"So, how are you feeling now?" I asked.

"I'm not so bad," he said. "The nurses in here are bloody marvellous. What's happened to you?"

"I've just broken a bone in my leg," I said. "It's bloody painful."

We chatted for a couple of minutes and then a hospital porter and a nurse arrived. The porter took the brakes off the trolley wheels and the nurse made the man comfortable.

"Do you see that man, there?" The nurse asked, pointing to me.

"Yes," said the man from Ryhope.

"He helped buy the machine that just pulled you round."

"Did he?" The man asked.

"That's the comedian, Bobby Knoxall," said the nurse. "And you've got him to thank for helping you breathe properly."

As the porter wheeled the trolley bed off, the man stuck his thumb into the air.

"Good on yer, Bobby, son," he said, smiling. "Good on yer. Keep it up."

The cost of the respiratory machine was a few thousand pounds, but the smile on that injured man's face was priceless. It was the first time I had seen the direct delivery of a service I had helped create, through the work I had done for charity.

The need for the machine was driven home to me when I had attended the hospital the previous year, again with an injury sustained during my acrobatic stage show. That time I had badly twisted my neck.

I set about staging a series of shows to help raise cash to buy the machine and later presented a cheque to the Mayor of Sunderland, Alderman Mrs Mary Miller. One of the shows was a 24-hour spectacular at The Manhattan Club in Sunderland during which all the artistes gave their services free of charge. The marathon started at 12noon and ended the following lunchtime, and hundreds of people came through the doors to see the acts and donate cash for the fund.

I had arranged and performed at one-off charity shows in the past, but the 24-hour marathon was certainly the biggest and most successful I was involved in. The show, in 1969, arranged just before my first summer tour in Jersey, set a trend for me that continued for the rest of my career.

By that time I had been a professional comedian for almost ten years and during that decade I had taken part in about 400 charity shows, raising tens of thousands of pounds. It would be difficult to put a headline figure on how much charity cash I have raised during my career spanning more than 50 years, but it must be upwards of a quarter of a million.

People have often asked me why I've done so much for charity and I've always found it difficult to answer that question. I suppose it's because I just like to help out where I can. I have never had any difficulty finding work – my comedy has taken me all over the world – and even when I was on the bones of my backside I knew I could always raise cash by doing a few clubs in my hometown area.

I have a talent for standing on stage and telling gags and people flock to watch me. Often I see the same faces in the audience that I have been entertaining for years, this hardcore following that have supported me since day one. It is these people who donate the charity cash, I'm just the vehicle that transports the cash from their pockets to the charitable cause.

In the early days my charitable efforts were one-off shows for specific causes, such as raising money to buy new equipment for the local hospital, or helping out at shows for the Newspaper Press Fund, alongside other club-land acts like The Dixelanders and Valtino. The biggest influence on me then, as far as fund-raising was concerned, was Tommy Nelson, who helped arrange many charity nights locally.

But even when my work took me abroad I would become involved in some charitable venture. In South Africa, along with other artistes, I helped raise a lot of cash for a children's orphanage.

One of the biggest influences on my charity work in recent years has been big Adrian Marshall, who regularly stages charity functions at The Alexandra in Grangetown, Sunderland, and always calls upon me to help out, by helping to provide the acts and acting as Master of Ceremonies.

Many people think that I, and the rest of the artistes, get paid for this, but the fact is we only ever get expenses, usually just a few pound for petrol.

Over recent years we have helped raise cash for a prosthetic limb for a young lad who lost a leg when he fell from the Wearmouth Bridge. The plight of a young lass called Hope Elliott, from Red House, Sunderland, who has a condition that has resulted in her having a disfigured face, touched the hearts of thousands of people across the North East and Adrian and I teamed up to do a show to raise what cash we could.

More recently I received a telephone call from the father of a young girl from Seaham, Rachel Spence, who has an inoperable brain tumour and had expressed the desire to swim with dolphins in Florida. Adrian and I arranged a show at The Alexandra and helped raise a few thousand pounds towards fulfilling the young girl's dream. Several Sunderland footballers donated items for auction and our guest speaker was big Jack Charlton.

One of my old pals, George Craig, who had built up one of the biggest charities in the North East, the Lazarus Foundation and the Lazarus Centre, the latter being a rehabilitation unit for recovering drug addicts and alcoholics, donated £2,000 to the cause and local businessman Dave Lawson pledged to make his villa in Florida available to the girl's family if they wished to stay there.

That's the thing I have always found with Sunderland people; they're always prepared to help others in need. I suppose it part of a Mackem's make-up. Sunderland people are naturally generous and naturally friendly. That's why I have always returned home from my travels across the globe, and that's why the majority of my charity work has been carried out in my home town.

*   *   *   *   *   *   *

My "Back Home" concert was something of a stage comeback for me, in my home territory. Singer Shaun Conley, who had recently auditioned in New York, was in fine voice and put on a great performance.

The event wasn't a charity night, just a tentative return to the stage, a kind of pre-cursor to me getting fully fit and fully back into work. I was dipping my toe into the water. The cameras were at the club to record material for the video I was bringing out and I felt fit enough to spend about 45 minutes on stage, going through my routine, and the audience lapped it up.

But I wanted more. I wanted to get fully back to work.

Chapter Twenty Three

I'M BACK!

The bright lights shone on to my face as I stood on the stage, microphone in hand, and looked towards the audience packing out the room at the Chilton Country Pub and Hotel in Fence Houses, near Sunderland. I could see all the familiar faces who had followed my career for more than 50 years, all looking towards the stage and waiting for me to launch into my routine.

I felt fitter now than I had for more than two years, physically and mentally. I looked smart and my brain was in top gear.

For me, this was not just another charity show fronted by Bobby Knoxall, it was the start of something special

I switched the microphone on.

"Good evening, ladies and gentlemen," I said. "My name is Bobby Knoxall, and I'm a comedian."

There was a ripple of laughter from the audience, but, at least for now, I didn't want a laugh.

"I want to be serious, just for one moment," I said.

"Eighteen months ago I was virtually told I was going to die. But I'm here, tonight, and I'm fighting fit.

"When I first entered show-business, one of my first shows was a charity show, raising cash for the local hospital, and it went well.

"Now, here I am, more than 50 years later, hosting another charity do. Isn't it strange how life can turn full circle?

"You see, I've been given a second chance at life, a second bite at the cherry, thanks to those wonderful surgeons at Sunderland Hospital

"I want to make the most of what little time I have left and in that time I can't think of doing anything better than helping to raise cash for what will be a children's hospice for Sunderland.

"I want to thank you all for your support; the support you have given me tonight, and, more than that, the support you have given me over the past 50 years."

No one in the audience laughed, they all just stood up from their seats, one by one, and launched into applause.

I stood on the stage feeling slightly embarrassed, as the applause rang in my ears for more than one minute. For the first time in my life I did not know where to put my face.

"Cease!" I said, using the old catchphrase I used on radio in South Africa so many times.

"Cease!"

Eventually, the spontaneous round of applause subsided and people began to take their seats.

I looked at one woman in the audience.

"You thought I was dead, didn't you missus?"

She looked rather shocked.

"Well, I'm not," I said. "And I'd like to tell you and everyone else in the audience one thing. Bobby Knoxall is back!"

The audience burst into applause again, and soon I was able to start my act.

The *Sunderland Echo's* Children of Courage Appeal was a charitable cause close to my heart, because I had been at death's door. I was approached by a member of the editorial staff at the *Echo* who asked me if I would be willing to do a series of charity shows to help raise cash towards the building of a £5million Children's Hospice in Sunderland. I jumped at the opportunity, as I thought this would probably me my last chance to do something worthwhile for the hometown I loved so much.

The hospice will provide much needed care for children with life-threatening illnesses and, as far as I was concerned, if I could play a part in raising some cash for the very worthwhile effort, I was only too willing to do so. The hospice will be there, long after I am gone.

With the help of Matt Roseberry, an old friend who owns the Chilton Country Pub and many other pubs, clubs and hotels, and with the help of other friends, Sammy Doran, at The Burton House pub in Sunderland city centre, Bill Tipling and John Hutchinson at the Ivy Leaf Club in Hendon, big Adrian Marshall at The Alexandra in Grangetown, my nephew Darren McKenna, at the Red House Workmen's Club, and other contacts within the local pub and club scene, Bobby Knoxall's Chuckles for Charity Roadshow 2003 hit the road.

The *Echo* was giving the Roadshow as much publicity as possible and my friend Joe Foster was helping me to secure the singers, comedians and musicians who would give their services for free.

The *Echo* appeal was part of the bigger fundraising drive to reach the £5million target to build Grace House. The whole fundraising drive was spearheaded by North East television and radio personality Kathy Secker, whom Matt Roseberry and I met at the *Echo's* office in Pennywell to outline what we were planning to do. Kathy was delighted with the Roadshow idea.

Many acts were giving their services free of charge for the roadshow, among them an up-and-coming young comedian from Redcar, Cleveland, Chris McGlade. I have always rated Chris who, like me, has raised a lot of cash for charity.

Other acts, generously giving their time and services free of charge, and all from the East End of Sunderland, were talented guitarist Bobby Carlisle and terrific singing duo Dolimix.

For me it was fitting that, more than 50 years on since doing my first charity shows, here I was now involved in the longest-running series of fundraising shows I had ever been involved in.

After my introduction at The Chilton on came the man with the big voice, Shaun Conley, and the first of the roadshows was very much up and running.

I took a seat and reached into my jacket pocket for my cigarettes. I hadn't worn that jacket since my "Back Home" do at the River Wear Social Club a few weeks earlier.

I pulled out a letter which had been handed to me at the River Wear. I had forgotten it was there.

The letter had a five pound note attached to it and a brief message which read: *"Please accept a couple of pints on me in appreciation of all the belly laughs over the years you have given me and the people in the North East."*

The letter read:

"Just a few lines to wish you a very successful night, and every success with your video.

I have been a great fan of yours, even before you went on stage. I'm talking about the 50s, when every pub in Sunderland had a piano and you and I were only teenagers.

I always knew I was in for a good night when I saw you in a pub (as a customer). I remember one night when you danced on the pub's mantelpiece and jumped off and done the splits.

I could never get near you to speak, as you always had a crowd around you. But they were great days.

If I ever was to meet you, Bob, the question I'd like to ask you is, if you could live your life over, would you change anything?

I'm sorry I won't be at your show tonight, as I will be out of town, but maybe it's just as well because the last time I saw you I had to walk out in the middle, I was laughing so much I thought I was going to die.

I wish you a long, healthy and happy life and please don't ever think of retiring, as you keep our memories of the North East alive."

The letter was signed simply Bryan, of Silksworth, Sunderland, and as I sat in my seat at The Chilton, I pondered on the question Bryan asked.

If I could live my life over, would I change anything?

I had gone from the abject poverty of the East End of Sunderland to earning thousands in some of the best hotels in the world, having toured Africa, the Middle East, the Far East, a short tour of Australia, jetted off to Las Vegas and entertained the troops in Italy. I had travelled to Canada and all over Europe.

I had earned and blown a fortune on booze, cigarettes, gambling and women (I never kept records but I must have bedded at least 200 beautiful women in my time).

I had met and worked with some of the world's greatest stars; Charlton Heston, Rocky Marciano, Ella Fitzgerald, Acker Bilk, Johnny Mathis, Roy Orbison, Marti Wilde, Marti Caine and many, many, more.

I had worked alongside such top comedians as Tommy Cooper, Les Dawson, Freddie Starr, Bob Monkhouse, my old mate Mike Reid, Ken Dodd, Dave Allen and many other household-name comics who launched glittering careers in television.

I had never made it in television myself and, despite promises made by others that I could become a millionaire, I had chosen my own path in life and ended up skint.

I had made friends with some of the top sporting stars in the world of boxing and football and had the names and personal telephone numbers of many in my little contacts book.

I had met some of Britain's top villains, such as Frankie Fraser and the Kray Twins, and had associations with some of the biggest villains and hard cases in the North East, some of whom were later jailed for everything from fraud to murder. They say if you lie with dogs you catch fleas, but despite my associations with villains, I had never been sent to jail.

I had been a rebel, a hell-raiser, had kicked seven bells out of many who challenged me, I had floored some of my agents and put other people in hospital and had downed enough Bacardi and coke to fill a tanker.

I had helped raise tens of thousands of pounds for local charities. With my help people were treated on new equipment bought for Sunderland General Hospital, a young, terminally ill girl was on her way to fulfil her dream of swimming with dolphins, and a painfully facially disfigured young girl was receiving the best medical treatment in the world. It wasn't all down to me – many hundreds of others had also raised thousands for these worthwhile causes – but what I had done was contributed, given something back to the community which had given me so much over the years. That meant more to me than any standing ovation, or any club-land award.

I had met and worked with some of the most charismatic entertainers the world had ever known.

And throughout it all, the friends I had made during my days as a barrow boy and in my early teens elsewhere, were still my friends, and I knew that if I needed them, they were there. These were genuine friendships that money just can't buy.

On top of all that I had fathered eight fantastic children, four to my first marriage and four to my second, and I was married to the most beautiful woman I had ever met in my life.

Now, for the first time in more than two years, I was in reasonable health.

I had had more than £2 million through my hands during a career that had taken me to the four corners of the globe. And yet I was still living with my family in a two-bedroom council house in my hometown of Sunderland.

I had met many sad and lonely millionaires who knew the cost of everything but the value of nothing and many famous stars whose lives had become empty shells once they had disappeared from the limelight, many had sank into the depths of despair living shallow lives propped up by alcohol or drugs.

I had many things that money couldn't buy; my family, my friends, my fans, my hometown, the gift of comedy and laughter ... and my second chance at life.

I had 20 Embassy Regal king size, my lighter, my car keys, and seven pounds and fifty pence in my pocket. After 50 years in show-business, that was the sum total of my capital assets.

But despite that, tonight, I felt richer than any multi-millionaire.

If I had my life to live over, would I change anything?

The answer, in short, Bryan, is no.